# Lest Devon Forgets

*The unveiling of Silverton's monument, 23 April 1922.*

# Lest Devon Forgets

## Service, Sacrifice and the
## Creation of Great War Memorials

## Todd Gray

THE
MINT
PRESS

First published in Great Britain by
The Mint Press, 2010

© Todd Gray 2010

ISBN 978-1-903356-56-2

Cataloguing in Publication Data
CIP record for this title is available from the British Library

The Mint Press
Taddyforde House South
Taddyforde Estate
New North Road
Exeter, Devon
England EX4 4AT

Typeset by Kestrel Data
Cover design by Delphine Jones

Printed and bound in Great Britain
by Short Run Press Ltd, Exeter

# CONTENTS

*For Meg and Richard*

'God of our father, known of old
Lord of our far flung battle line
Beneath Whose awful Hand we hold
Dominion over palm and pine
Lord God of Hosts, be with us yet,
Lest we forget, lest we forget!'

Rudyard Kipling, Recessional, 1897

# PREFACE

My interest in war memorials began in 1999 when I saw one
in a former Soviet Republic. It provoked me to think about
how markedly different it was to any I had seen in Devon.
Since then I have been collecting and cataloguing information
on those that were erected across the county. What has
gradually emerged is an extraordinary network of some two
thousand unique memorials.[1] I suspected there may be that
many but only through travelling the length and breadth of
the countryside does it become apparent how individual each
one is. Over the last few years I have visited nearly every of
the county's ancient 450 Anglican churches and many of the
Victorian ones as well as some of the Free Churches. I have
also endeavoured to view every communal monument. What
has made this tour so extraordinary is discovering that no
two memorials are the same. This is probably the case across
the country but I have been able to confirm that each Devon
monument is unique and that they reflect the people and
places memorialised.

Devon has had many people look at particular village
war memorials and a few researchers have looked across a
wide area but no one has been interested in how they were
created across the county.[2] It is this broader aspect that has
most intrigued me as I have explored the diverse variety of
memorials which reflect the impact the war had nearly one
hundred years ago.

I am deeply grateful to those friends and colleagues with whom I have travelled. I would like to thank Michael Clayson, Paul Cleave, Judith Cosford, Katrina & Ed Deacon, Carole & Ray Herbert, Lawrence Hunt, Brian & Elizabeth Jackson, David Kremer, Willow McFarlan, Olive Millward, Graham Naylor, Richard Parker, Graham & Jan Parnell, Trish Rodbourne, Reuben Rowe, Bob Vickery, Rob Ward and particularly Keith Stevens for their time, interest and patience. Church wardens and officers across Devon have opened their churches to allow me access to their war memorials and I am very grateful to them. I am also indebted to the staffs, too many to name individually, of the British Library at Colindale, Cookworthy Museum, Devon & Exeter Institution, Devon Record Office, Devonport Library, Exeter Cathedral Library, Ilfracombe Museum, Newton Abbot Town & GWR Museum, North Devon Athenaeum, Okehampton Library, Plymouth & West Devon Record Office, Plymouth Local Studies Library, Sidmouth Library, Tiverton Museum of Mid Devon Life, Torquay Local Studies Library, University of Exeter Main Library, and Westcountry Studies Library. I would like to thank Delphine Jones for her superb cover. Dr Tony Kelly and Dr Tim Reese offered useful criticisms for which I thank them. This study has been helped and furthered by the expertise and kindness of many people but any and all mistakes are my own.

Todd Gray, Exeter
1 October 2010

# INTRODUCTION

A visitor to the small village of Washfield near Tiverton
might notice today a wooden shelter in a corner of the modest
recreation ground. It is an unassuming building but is the only
one of its kind in Devon. It was erected as a war memorial
and the carved inscription announces 'The shelter was erected
to commemorate the men of Washfield who served abroad
during the Great War, 1914–1918'. For reasons unique unto
themselves, the people of Washfield created their own way,
unlike any other in Devon, to honour their men who returned
from war.

Like the villagers of Washfield, Devonians in every other
corner of the county were still in the midst of the Great
War when they began to discuss what the most appropriate
way was to mark the service of those who had gone abroad.
These discussions broadened to negotiations and eventually
culminated in an unparalleled network of memorials. Like
the rest of Britain Devonians were unknowingly creating sites
that became firstly the focus for community remembrance
of the Great War and then evolved as the meeting points for
honouring those who fought in all subsequent wars. Three
generations later these monuments are as relevant now as

1

1. *Washfield's shelter, one of Devon's unusual Great War memorials.
The tablet can be seen to the right.*

they originally were but they have become a ubiquitous part
of the landscape, so much so that they are generally ignored
and overlooked except during the Armistice Day celebrations.
There are few other man-made objects in the landscape that
can be found in every community across Devon. Red telephone
boxes, once a familiar sight, are now a rarity and perhaps
only Royal Mail post boxes are more commonplace. What
also makes war memorials unusual is that those which were
erected as crosses have, in one respect, taken the place of the
ancient preaching crosses that were once a common feature
but began to be pulled down in the early 1500s. Four hundred
years later we have this second network of crosses and many
of them are situated near to the sites of their predecessors.
However, whereas the medieval stones acted as a call to pray
to the Almighty these invoke a different moral obligation on
the passer-by. They implore the reader to pay homage to the

2. *A war memorial which has lost its dignity.*
*This alabaster tablet for a church in Barnstaple, was unveiled*
*by the Dean of Exeter in April 1920 in its position on the*
*west wall of the porch. This space is now used as a toilet.*

dead and emulate their example by exhibiting good behaviour. What they have in common is that both are reminders of self-sacrifice.

What is not generally known, or is at least under-appreciated, is that each community produced a unique monument. Each differs both in its form and dedication. Local discussions, often heated, produced a varied range of monuments that reflected local politics, class struggles, rivalries, religious tensions, taste and economics. Some became highly controversial but all were erected with local pride and usually with a great deal of fanfare and respectful commemoration. Many were produced locally by Devon craftsmen known only within a small area while others were created by local men who had established reputations across the country including Courtenay Pollock. Some men became eminent in their later years, including John Angel, while other work was by such national figures as Sir Reginald Blomfield, Sir Edwin Lutyens, William Macmillan, Henry Poole, Birnie Rhind, James Stevenson and Sir Charles Wheeler. Many are extraordinary pieces of art. Some memorials are relatively modest tributes while others, like those raised by the City of Exeter in Northernhay Park and by the Royal Navy on Plymouth Hoe, are works of considerable size and importance. Some small towns achieved monuments of great height: Chulmleigh's cross is fourteen feet high, Lynton's monument stands at twenty feet, Barnstaple's cross is twenty-one feet high and Exmouth's memorial is twenty-two feet high. Even so, these appear modest in comparison with Devon County Council's cross at thirty feet, Devonport's is no less than thirty-three and the Royal Navy's monument in Plymouth stands at over one hundred. Some villages created stunning stained-glass windows and others erected unusual and curious monuments that have survived nearly three generations later. Hundreds of private memorials were created by friends and family members and there were other types of private initiatives. One which is out of the ordinary is the Victory Club at Plymouth. This was an initiative of Lady

3. *Jacobstowe's monument, symbolic perhaps
of an eternal light.*

Astor and had a membership in 1924 of 400 children. Its aim was to train them in handicrafts and it was established as a war memorial.[3] Another distinctive memorial is the lamp placed in the churchyard by the parishioners of Jacobstowe. The history of the erection of these monuments is one made up of diverse individual influences and factors. Some small villages achieved extraordinary memorials while some towns, like Paignton, had to compromise their aspirations. Even the Dean of Exeter Cathedral had to admit defeat in his proposal to restore the Cloisters as a monument and quietly withdrew his plans.

There are fewer monuments today than there were nearly a century ago largely because of the destruction caused by the Second World War. Many of those which had been erected in churches in Exeter and Plymouth were destroyed as a result of the intensive bombing by the Germans. Others were lost in random attacks at Budleigh Salterton, Clyst St George and Aveton Giffard amongst others. Some which had been erected in secular buildings were also hit by Nazi bombs and reduced to rubble. It is ironic that memorials made to honour men who died fighting Germans in one war were then destroyed by their countrymen less than a generation later. Despite this loss in the early 1940s many hundreds survive.

The history of these monuments can often be told because many documents survive. These are generally found amongst parish papers and some are extraordinarily detailed. Local newspapers were also very interested and there are hundreds of news stories on the progress on monuments across Devon. Only occasionally are the reports slight such as with the unveiling of Holsworthy's memorial cross: the journalist at one local newspaper could not write a full report because he had left his notes behind on the train.[4]

Devon, like the rest of the country, experienced economic uncertainty in the immediate aftermath of the war. Its two cities were very different and had been for centuries. Plymouth, the largest of the two, was dominated by the navy and had some industry whereas Exeter was largely a retail centre with some light industry but benefiting from being the county's legal centre as well that of the diocese of Exeter. The memorials reflect their characters: Plymouth had the monuments to the Royal Navy and the Royal Marines while Exeter attracted those of the County Council and the Devonshire Regiment. The north and south coasts were highly dependent upon the summer holiday trade while rural Devon was a mix of pastoral and arable farming. The influx of migrants was strongest in the coastal communities than in the rural hinterland of Devon and the former had a more cosmopolitan air. Certainly Salcombe and Torquay had for generations attracted a wider range of new residents than say Sheepwash or Cheldon. Perhaps an indication of this can be found in the war memorials where some of the larger urban areas chose figurative and less traditional forms of monuments. It is also indicative of the diocese's leanings to High Church in some urban parishes that they were enveloped in Great War memorial frictions and controversies. It would be interesting to know if Devon had more of these than elsewhere.

The pressure for these monuments arose from within the communities themselves. There was a need to show gratitude to servicemen as well as a desire on the behalf of the bereaved to have a place to remember the dead, particularly given so many men were buried abroad.

Each community in Devon, like those across the country, had to decide what was appropriate to mark local service and sacrifice. The complexities in meeting unexpected and varying village sensibilities were explained by one Devonian who took a part in his war memorial. He wrote:

'So many people have asked me, since its erection outside the council school some weeks ago, whether it is a Victory Cross or a Memorial to the Fallen that I think some explanation may be needed. When the question of a Parish War Memorial was first raised many of us felt that it could take no better or more

7

4. *Inwardleigh's stone monument which aroused controversy when it was erected.*

useful form than a village hall for entertainments, dances, etc. which is badly needed in this parish, but, as this suggestion was strongly opposed by those who disapprove of recreation (particularly dancing) for our young people, the project fell through.

It was then proposed that a granite cross should be put in the churchyard in memory of the five men who lost their lives in the war but some people objected to the churchyard being the chosen spot, instead of the chapel burying ground. So, to meet the case, somebody suggested that it should be erected outside the school, but the bereaved families and many others felt that this rough, unhallowed spot was one of the last places in which to perpetuate the memory of our living dead, especially as arrangements had already been made to place a marble tablet inside the church in memory of these men.

As, however, there seemed to be a general desire for a granite cross, but the site chosen for it was unsuitable for a memorial, I suggested that the stone be erected solely in commemoration of the cessation of hostilities , and should bear the names of all those from this parish who fought to secure Peace for us.

This proposal being agreed to, the stone was ordered and erected, and Easter Monday having been chosen for its unveiling, most people were looking forward to a day of general rejoicing, but, to our amazement, we are now given to understand it is a 'Memorial to the Fallen', and that our annual Easter Monday dance, which will take place, as usual, in the evening, is in the nature of an insult to the dead, and quite out of place, under the circumstances.

In justice to the ex-Servicemen and others responsible for this dance, who would be the last to wish to dishonour in any way those men who gave their lives for their country, I must strongly repudiate this suggestion, and point out that no mention is made of the word 'memorial' on the stone itself which is inscribed thus

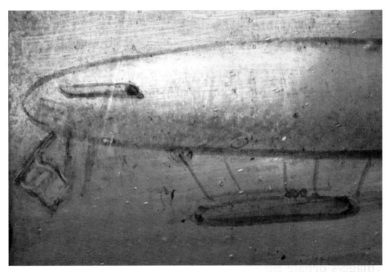

5–6. *Typical of the memorials that can be found across Devon is the Great War stained glass window at Pyworthy which features this airplane and airship.*

*'Lest we forget*

*This stone is erected by the parishioners as a lasting*
*tribute to those who responded to the call of duty in the*
*Great War, 1914–1918'*

The names of the forty men who served following in
alphabetical order, and as 35 of the 40 men whose names it
bears are fortunately alive and well, I fail to see how the stone
can rightly be described as a memorial or why the dance in the
evening is in any way out of place.'[5]

This small village in mid-Devon on the northern edges of
Dartmoor shared many of the same issues that arose in other
villages over their war memorials: religious tensions arose and
villagers debate the form, location and name of monuments
as well as what and who should be commemorated. Other
issues came to the fore and each was dependent upon local
considerations and sensibilities. Inwardleigh was, in some
respects, like the rest of Devon.

Nearly three generations have passed since the network of
Devon's war memorials was erected. They exist, in all their
poignancy, pathos and creative glory, waiting to be noticed.

## ONE

# THE PUBLIC APPETITE
# FOR MEMORIALS

As many as two thousand Great War memorials were created in Devon. The impetus came from emulating those then being erected in London. In Devon they began to appear during the war itself: Exeter had one outside the parish church of St Olave as early as in January 1917 and it was then claimed to be the second in the West Country.[6] However, the rush began following the appearance of the Cenotaph in London in the summer of 1919. Devon, like the rest of the country, sought to imitate this national memorial and shortly afterwards many hundreds of monuments sprang up across the Devon landscape. In effect, the lead came from national government but the impetus sprang up within local communities.

Lutyen's Cenotaph set the standard; within weeks a Teignmouth resident suggested that the town's memorial, which was to be placed in the public area known as the Dene, should not take the form of a cross but instead be a replica of the Cenotaph. He thought would be 'a more suitable and appropriate memorial both in regard to its object and surroundings'. Other Devonians also wanted their version of the Cenotaph[7] including at Hatherleigh where the war memorial committee agreed to erect one in 1920.[8] However, it soon became apparent that cenotaphs were inappropriate for many communities for varying reasons. Other practical forms of remembrance had to be found that would express both grief and gratitude.

Sombre remembrance ceremonies were held during the conflict itself but it was the truce of November 1918 that galvanised the public to hold commemoration events. At first these were held in churches and civic spaces but increasingly, as the monuments appeared, the ceremonies took place alongside the new memorial. In effect, the monuments were erected to remember those who fought in the war but the ceremonies became annual events which were fashioned around these new memorials. The monuments and their ceremonies were unparalleled in the country's history in that they became a part of the annual life of every British town and city and nearly every village. Although probably unaware of it, they were creating communal centres of grief which would last far beyond the lives of those who lived through the war. Moreover, members of all denominations could meet at those places on equal terms.

The majority of memorials in Devon were created in 1920 and 1921. The more expensive monuments were generally later than the smaller and less costly village memorials but this was not always the case. The most expensive was the Victory Wing to the Devon & Exeter Hospital: it cost £35,000.

It took several years for local committees to be organised, for them to agree on the form of the memorial, to raise the funds, for the work to be commissioned and executed, and finally for the unveiling to the public. There were also delays in finding suitable sites and, within churches, in obtaining permission to erect them. The committee at Abbotskerswell outside Newton Abbot was unanimous in its opinion that had the members realised the obstacles in placing a tablet inside a church they would have taken it elsewhere. They agreed not to fund any further work inside the church and asked the cleric

## Devon's leading war memorials

| Creator | Form | Site | Date of Unveiling |
|---|---|---|---|
| Crediton Urban District Council | Recreation Gd | Crediton | uncertain |
| Torquay Borough | Pylon | Torquay | 23 April 1921 |
| Devon County Council | Cross | Exeter | 16 May 1921 |
| Devonshire Regiment | Figure | Exeter | 26 June 1921 |
| Paignton Urban District Council | Obelisk | Paignton | 29 June 1921 |
| Crediton private individuals | Organ | Crediton | 16 November 1921 |
| Newton Abbot Urban District Council | Column | Newton Abbot | 23 July 1922 |
| Various | Hospital Wing | Exeter | June 1922 |
| Barnstaple Borough | Cross | Barnstaple | 15 October 1922 |
| Devonport | Cross | Devonport | 14 March 1923 |
| Crediton Urban District Council | 'Shelter' | Crediton | 16 May 1923 |
| City of Plymouth | Figure | Plymouth | 28 May 1923 |
| City of Exeter | Figures | Exeter | 24 July 1923 |
| Lynton Urban District Council | Column | Lynton | 1 January 1924 |
| Imperial War Graves Commission | Column | Plymouth | 29 July 1924 |
| Ilfracombe Urban District Council | Column | Ilfracombe | 11 November 1924 |
| Kingsbridge Urban District Council | Figure | Kingsbridge | 15 November 1925 |
| Various | Hospital | Okehampton | 20 October 1926 |
| Tiverton Borough | Library | Tiverton | c.1929 |

to register their disappointment with the Registrar.[9] Some
committees found their job exasperating. One monument
which proved particularly problematic to finish was that for
the City of Plymouth. At the unveiling it was admitted:

'It has been a hard, almost a heroic, fight to win for the
fallen 2,000 the recognition that was their due. It was belated

7. *Barnstaple's civic monument which was erected following
a difficult campaign to raise the funds.*

and delayed until hearts had hardened and grief has almost crystallized into cynicism. It will never be known, it is not desirable that it should ever be known, how stern a task has for four years faced the War Memorial Committee, and with what patience and faith the leaders of the committee have worked to bring an almost hope-abandoned scheme to consummation'.

Perhaps it helped that one of the committee was an 'arch-optimist'.[10] The number of memorials overwhelmed local masons and builders. Herbert Read, one of Exeter's leading ecclesiastical craftsmen, wrote to one committee in 1919 that he was exceedingly busy[11] and he told another, that at Salcombe Regis, to stop being 'impetuous'. They felt the work was overdue but he pointed out that he had 'foolishly' put their cross ahead of those from other parishes. He was, he said, under great pressure to complete war memorials and other parishes were waiting longer because Salcombe Regis had jumped their place in the queue.[12] This profusion of war monuments was noted by one Devon newspaper in the spring of 1919. It claimed 'every town and even village with any pretensions to patriotism is undergoing something like panic in the attempt to devise and arrange a novel and fitting form of war memorial.'[13] Another carver, John Northcott of Ashwater, also commented in 1922 that he was overwhelmed by requests to do war memorials.[14] At least he was not held up by workers' strikes. In 1920 four local stone carving firms had their employees refuse to work for nearly a month and it took mediation talks to reach an agreement. Herbert Read of Exeter, Harry Hems & Sons of Exeter, Wippells & Co. of Exeter and Dart & Francis of Crediton all had men on strike. The men placed their own advert:

'Wanted – first class wood and stone carvers to work on memorials to the glorious dead – at the lowest wage in England'.

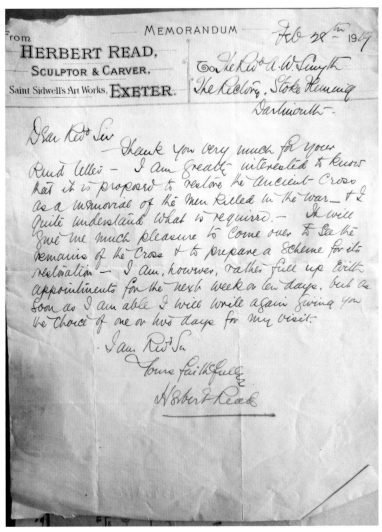

8. *A letter from Herbert Read providing advice on a war memorial.*

In Exeter they were paid one shilling and six pence an hour which was the lowest wage in Devon. An agreement was later reached to increase their pay and promise not to victimise the men.[15] Paignton's obelisk was delayed because of two strikes at the Dartmoor quarry in 1920 and 1921.[16] Inflation during the war prompted industrial action just as the memorials were being created. The demand for monuments could not be instantly met by the few available masons and other craftsmen. Courtney Pollock, who was trying to finish the war memorial for Newton Abbot, complained that he was even considering hiring German workers because he could not get any who were British. He informed the town council he had put their war memorial before all others but sculptors and foundries were 'choked' with war memorial commissions. Pollock urged Newton Abbot's committee to appreciate the chaotic condition of Britain and informed them he was not a conjurer and could not supply a delivery date for their monument.[17]

From 1919 the 11th of November became the focus for annual commemoration ceremonies. At Teignmouth that year, as in the rest of Devon, a message from King George V was published.

'I believe that my people in every part of the Empire fervently wish to perpetuate the memory of that great deliverance and of those who laid down their lives to achieve it. To afford an opportunity for the universal expression of this feeling, it is my desire and hope that at the hour when the armistice came into force – the eleventh hour of the eleventh day of the eleventh month – there may be for the brief space of two minutes a complete suspension of all our normal activities. During that time, except in the rare cases where this may be impracticable, all work, all sound, and all locomotion should cease, so that in perfect stillness the thoughts of everyone may be concentrated in reverent remembrance of the glorious dead'.

The local newspaper duly announced that the 'hooter' at the Teignmouth Steam Laundry would sound at eleven and then two minutes later.[18] The silence was observed across Devon and as monuments began to appear on the landscape people gathered there together.

There were also other dates. The 4th of August, the anniversary of when war was declared, had been a day of national prayer from 1915. In 1918, the fifth year of war, it was titled Remembrance Day. Solemn services were held throughout the country and more than ten thousand people filled Exeter Cathedral for each service.[19] On the 20th of May 1923 at least 20,000 Plymothians celebrated their own Remembrance Day with a service on the Hoe.[20] Another ceremonial date was Comrades Sunday, in July, when former servicemen marched and laid wreaths. These dates in the calendar eventually gave way to November 11 as the prime date of remembrance and the war memorials also took over from churches as the sites for homage.

Armistice Day was instantly popular. In 1920 Bradninch was one of the many Devon communities to suspend all activity. Local people gathered at their new war memorial cross, the bells were tolled 52 times to individually mark the 52 local men who had lost their lives, flags were flown at half-mast, the hooters of the paper mills were blown and in the distance could be heard the booming of a cannon.[21] Likewise at Brentor in West Devon there was a gathering at their war memorial: children processed to the cross where they laid flowers and the vicar held a service.[22] Similar events were held across the country on the first anniversary of the Peace Treaty and in all subsequent years.

The memorials of the Great War were not without precedent. Monuments to mark individual war service was a longstanding practice but it was not until the South African wars of the late-nineteenth and early-twentieth-centuries that memorials of various shapes and forms began to become more commonplace. One which is similar to the Great War memorials was erected at Bradninch. It was inscribed 'To the glory of God and in honour of four Bradninch men who gave their lives for their king and country in the South African war, 1899–1902'. Another is for four men in the Anglican church at Dalwood: 'to the glory of God and in pious memory of . . . who gave their lives for England in the Boer War, 1899–1902'. In Exeter Cathedral there are marble tablets with the names of several hundred local men. A great stained glass window was also erected. Dozens of other memorials were created across the county to mark the deaths of other men.

One of the most unusual, and relevant to the Great War, was erected at Filleigh near South Molton. This granite Latin cross was originally made to honour the memory of Lionel H. D. Fortescue of Castle Hill. He had died in 1900 at Diamond Hill in South Africa where he was buried. The cross was subsequently used to record the names of other family members who died in the Great War as well as other men of the parish and of those who died in the Second World War as well. It would be easy to assume this was originally a Great War cross.[23]

Even so, the number of South African memorials was, within twenty years, dwarfed by those erected for the First World War. This was partly due to the higher number of local men and women who served but it was the number of deaths, more than eleven thousand, which made the question of raising a memorial relevant to nearly every Devon community. Only a handful of parishes did not have residents who lost their lives in the war. The effect of the deaths could be disproportionate. At Ashprington sixteen members of the football club enlisted together but only three returned home[24] and at Harbertonford six of the nine local men who died had worked together in the mills.[25] At East Down, in north-east Devon, the cross commemorates the deaths of four men. Two of them were A. E. Ashton and W. Ashton, father and son.[26] A tablet in the Anglican church at Tamerton Foliot near Plymouth notes the deaths of another father and son only eight months apart.

9. *The memorial cross erected to honour Lionel Fortescue of Castle Hill who died in South Africa. Names were subsequently added from the First and Second World Wars.*

Thorverton was not unusual in that amongst the parishioners were a couple who had lost three sons.[27] There are similar stories for every part of Devon. The unprecedented number of dead and wounded servicemen moved people to show gratitude. They also knew that across the country fellow citizens were similarly attempting the same. In 1921 Devon County Council produced an official list of the 11,796 local men and women who died for their country. They were recorded under their home parish and the list was produced as a bound volume which was unveiled by the Prince of Wales at Exeter. Unfortunately few of these lists tally with the names on community memorials because a different criterion was used. For instance, Shillingford St George has no war dead according to the county list and yet it erected a tablet which honours eight local men. These men were either listed as resident elsewhere by Devon County Council or were omitted in error. Many parishes also produced books of their war dead. One of the most detailed is that of Heavitree near Exeter.[28] For Alfred Sidney Radford it recorded:

> 51 Victor Street
> Royal Navy – HMS Vala
> Rank – Leading Seaman
> Decoration – Distinguished Service Medal
> Ship lost and all crew drowned 7/8/17

Of Alfred Lionel Laver it noted:

> 21 Cross Park Terrace
> Regiment – 1st County of London Yeomanry
> Rank – Lance Corporal
> Killed in action while scouting in Gallipoli 1/9/1915

The book contains similar details of all the other men and women who died from Heavitree.

There appears to have been a widespread yearning to mark

these deaths and service; every Devon newspaper showed public support by featuring positive news stories as well as letters to the editors about movements to erect memorials. The Lord Lieutenant said in 1920 that there was nothing more striking than the generous zeal with which Devonians had stirred themselves to erect monuments during the previous two years.[29] In Plympton St Maurice there were complaints of an insufficient number of war memorials: the only one was the wall tablet inside the church. Following Remembrance Day in 1922, four years after the cessation of hostilities, *The Illustrated Weekly Western News* highlighted how unsatisfactory it was for wreaths to be placed around a cross which was unconnected with the war. It noted:

'it must be a grief to those who lost their loved ones on the battlefield or sea that they are denied the privilege granted in nearly every other village in the land of placing their wreaths on a spot reverenced by the whole population'.[30]

A monument was duly erected at the entrance to the Castle Green two years later.[31] The monuments appear to have been erected with genuine feelings of not just patriotism but a widespread sense of debt to the men, and women, who served abroad.

It became important that these war memorials provided a communal place which grieving family and friends could visit. This was particularly so for those with loved ones who had been buried overseas: an inability to visit foreign graves gave memorials an important and lasting place in the personal grieving process. This can be seen for another Devon community, that of Clovelly, where only four of their dead were brought back for burial in the village: the rest of the men remained where they died in France, Belgium and Palestine as well as on an Aegean island, Wales, Ireland and America. Two were lost at sea.[32] *The Illustrated Weekly Western News* had also made a second point: the memorials validated the

10. *The monument put up at Plympton St Maurice near the Castle.*

11. *Uplyme's cross, one of the few Great War trophies left on public display in Devon.*

deaths of loved ones in that they publicly proclaimed that the sacrifices were honoured.

Sufficient access to the war memorial was an issue raised at a public meeting in Colyton in 1920. The vicar suggested it was inappropriate for the gates to be locked so as to limit relatives' visits. One man said 'throw the gates open and we will look after the cross'. The meeting unanimously agreed with him.[33]

There were also voices against memorials. A war trophy at Lynton was thrown from the town hall thirty feet over the cliffs on Christmas morning 1920. It was said that the gift of the German field gun was unpopular and a previous attempt on the fifth of November had failed. One newspaper reported many residents thought this was 'a case of good riddance'. In 1920 Teignmouth also acquired a German field gun but not long after it was sited residents of Regent Street asked for it to be removed because 'the gun was a constant reminder of sorrow to those who had lost relatives in the war'.[34] These war trophies were given to acknowledge the war contribution of communities but may also have been seen not just as unnecessary but as a triumphant spoil of war. A woman in Walkhampton objected to the placing of the war memorial itself near her home: she wrote to her district council complaining that it would be a great eyesore and 'nothing but a huge tombstone to look out upon'.[35] Similar comments can be found across Devon but these are rare compared to the number supportive of the movement.

# TWO

# CREATING THE MEMORIALS

The creation of the monuments involved tens of thousands of individuals who worked either on their own accord or were organised collectively in over a thousand groups. They all individually learned, probably independently of other individuals or groups, what erecting a war memorial entailed.

While a diverse range of individuals and bodies created memorials the majority are sited in religious buildings or in their grounds. Of them the Church of England houses more memorials than any other religious group but others include the Baptists, Methodists, Congregationalists, Roman Catholics and Jews. No war memorials have yet been found in Devon for the Salvationists, Pentecostals, Plymouth Brethren, Society of Friends, Seventh Day Adventists, Muslims or Hindus but they may exist. Villages, towns and cities also organised hundreds of memorials as did private individuals, businesses, clubs and schools. The latter are the ones least seen as they are often in privately-owned buildings. A tablet in the lodge room of the Ilfracombe Loyal Combined Lodge of Oddfellows is typical of those for private groups[36] as is that for St John's Ambulance in Exeter.[37] Public buildings also have memorials

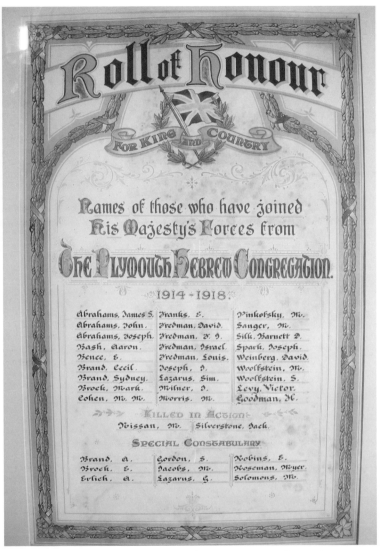

12. *The Roll of Honour at the Synagogue in Plymouth.*

including post offices, like that at Newton Abbot which in 1920 erected a monument,[38] as do the local police forces. Private companies, like Great Western Railway, have their memorials and countless others hang on the walls of other buildings or stand in the landscape.

Not all were erected to mark war service but were intended to commemorate victory or peace. The memorial clock at Coldridge, for example, was determinedly called a Peace Memorial.[39] Likewise the plot of land which was enclosed as a garden in Germansweek was dedicated 'in commemoration of peace 1919'. That year the parishioners of Alwington near Bideford decided to erect a cross as a war memorial and a hall as a peace memorial.[40] At Instow there was agreement that a cross should be erected in the churchyard to remember the fallen and that a separate Victory memorial was to be placed at the Quay.[41] The east window in one Devonport church had a unique inscription: it was 'erected by the members of this church to perpetuate the signing of Armistice and in grateful recognition of the sacrifices made by all ranks for the peace of Europe'.[42] Across Devon there are many other monuments which were not intended to mark war.

In every corner of Devon committees were formed. In the villages they were generally chaired by the Anglican cleric or another local worthy. The members were generally prominent people and few demobilised servicemen appear to have been asked to serve. The committee at Bideford comprised as many as thirty members but most were much smaller.[43] The members made decisions which were generally reported in public meetings but democracy was not always followed and sometimes charges of elitism were levelled at those in charge. At Paignton there were attempts to allow subscribers to decide the form of the monument but the committee refused to give up any power.[44] Dawlish was one place where the committee was criticised for not consulting or including the public in its plans. There were also criticisms at Dawlish over insufficient consultation of former servicemen or their families[45] but in many parishes strenuous efforts were made to canvas their opinions. This was notable at Holsworthy where the committee had decided to erect the memorial in the cattle market but reconsidered so that the relatives could be consulted.[46] At Churston Ferrers the committee wrote to surviving family and asked for their permission to place the names of the dead on the cross.[47]

However, the lack of consultation produced a reaction in Stoke Fleming near Dartmouth. Twenty-nine relatives and friends of the sixteen dead servicemen felt so strongly about the inscription that they petitioned the committee:

'We do not feel the memorial to these men could be rightly complete without some record of the Hope and Faith which we trust was their Succour, and must be our comfort, and we very earnestly beg that the committee will reconsider their decision'.

Another three parishioners admonished the committee for not consulting the bereaved. Nevertheless, their wishes were ignored and no text was added to the cross. They, along with designer, felt that it would take away from the aesthetics. [48]

Not surprisingly, committees were the focus for various political machinations. At Bideford it was agreed, at the urging of the local branch of the Federation for Discharged and Demobilised Sailors and Soldiers that no member would be eligible if he was a conscientious objector or an employer who refused to reinstate a serviceman to his pre-war job.[49]

Minutes of meetings held in the north-west Devon parish of Parkham show the difficulties and complexities in meeting varying needs and expectations. A public meeting was held in 1919 and various schemes were suggested including erecting monuments in the village green and Anglican churchyard as well as a clock in the church tower. Fifty-seven villagers voted for the winning proposal of a memorial on the green and all appeared to be straightforward. However, it was at a

Foxhill,

Galmpton,

Churston Ferrers .

16th April, 1919 .

Dear Sir or Madam,

CHURSTON PARISH WAR MEMORIAL .

A memorial for those of this parish who have fallen in the
Great War has been decided upon . The Committee are desirous
of perpetuating their memory by having their names inscribed
on a Memorial Cross to be erected on the Warborough Common.  As
your          has fallen in the service of his country the
Committee wish to know if you have any objection to his name
being recorded on the Memorial Cross .

If you have none, kindly let me have his correct name,
regiment and rank so as to have an accurate record .

It is proposed to engrave on the cross in addition to the names
of those fallen, the following inscription .

---

"Erected by the Parishioners of Churston Ferrers in grateful
remembrance of those from this parish who fell in the great
War 1914-19".

"Their memory liveth for ever" .

Yours truly,

HAYNE SMITH,

Hon . Secty .

13. *A committee attempting to consult the bereaved.*

subsequent committee meeting that brought out the disparate
and individual sensitivities. A letter was read from a woman
who had lost two sons in the war. She wrote that a cross,
similar to that which had been erected in France over her son's
grave, was being erected privately. It would be positioned in
the churchyard so that its shadow would pass over the graves

of the only three men who had died in the war and were buried at home. She wrote that of the scheme to erect a monument in the green 'it could not be thought of'. The rector revealed he had discussed with the returned men another idea, his own, which was to erect a memorial to them either as a brass tablet in the church or as a memorial on Beacon Hill. He had a mixed response. Another committee member questioned erecting a monument to the living and pointed out returned servicemen had been given 'a good feed and jollification'. He and another man wanted consensus within the village. A returned soldier said that 'he could speak from experience with the boys in the trenches that their only thought was of home and he considered the most suitable place for the memorial was the churchyard'. The committee then voted to drop their plans and 'leave it to private enterprise to erect one if they so wished'.[50] Two months later the private cross was erected. It was inscribed:

'In loving memory of our dear boys, 1914–1919. We their relatives and friends in Parkham place this monument here Christmas 1919, F. B. Washed ashore at Peppercombe June 1918'

A slate tablet was also later erected. On it was written:

'Not to be forgotten, 1914 – 1919, three fallen heroes rest in this churchyard near the cross raised in honour of our glorious dead. The church porch holds the record of our victorious returned. Thanks be to God'.

In addition to the cross an extraordinarily elaborate wall tablet was later placed in the church porch; it is more detailed than nearly any other in Devon. The brass lists each man by his months of service and where they served. Perhaps still smarting from the rebuff of the relatives, those that erected the memorial had it inscribed 'Some civilian admirers of the splendid services of our returned heroes gratefully place here

**Salcombe Regis Memorial and Thank=Offering.**

Please state:—

(1) The sum you wish to promise to both objects, or separately?

(2) Whether you prefer to pay in instalments? If so when?

(3) Any suggestions you have to make.

| Name | Amount Promised | No. of Instalments if any | When Payable | Suggestions |
|------|-----------------|---------------------------|--------------|-------------|
| Sir Norman and Lady Lockyer | £2.2.0 | | when the Cross is put up. | if the granite Cross is decided on. |

14. *Subscription slip at Salcombe Regis which allowed money to be given for a tablet, cross or memorial room.*

the record of the men connected with Parkham'. A photographic record of the men was also placed in the Anglican church.

The deliberations of the committee in the small East Devon parish of Salcombe Regis show how idealistic the aims could be. They decided to erect a roll of honour of those that served, a stone cross to mark those that died and a village hall or room as a memorial of thanksgiving for peace.[51] In the end they were not able to fulfil all their plans. Other groups were likewise too ambitious in their initial ideas but some places, like Crediton, managed to erect several significant memorials.

Stirring patriotic speeches were a hallmark of the public meetings. Possibly this was done to enthuse the audience but it appears that occasionally it was simple grandstanding. Often the speeches used the rhetoric of patriotism and were sometimes excessively jingoistic. For instance the chairman of the committee at Harberton near Totnes made an emotional speech. He said:

'In order to win this victory they had lost their bravest and dearest in the terrible struggle with a savage and relentless enemy, who used the whole of their high education and their great scientific knowledge in the cause of cruel, ruthless, diabolical and senseless slaughter. To this end they made the earth a shambles, and even the bottom of the sea a graveyard, not only with the recognised weapons of former wars as shell, shot and sword, but with satanic liquid fire, which shrivelled up the young heroes' very vitals, and deadly poisonous gas which corroded their brave young hearts and lungs. Women and children were tormented worse than by wild Indians, and night after night high explosives were rained down on their homes, which ground their loved ones to death and destruction, even to their very bones. The valour of the deceased sons braved all these dangers, and, by the blessing of God, defeated this bloodthirsty and outrageous enemy. They died that they may live, for had the Germans won the war, not one of them would be alive now, except as slaves, beasts of burden or helots [serfs]. They had to thank God they were spared this degradation, and not like the suffering Belgians and French obliged to witness the ravishing and outrage on their daughters and the hellish assassinations and tortures on their wives and children'.[52]

There was often an appearance of unanimity but discontent is often evident in the reporting.[53] The meetings sometimes gave vent to rancorous feelings. Chagford's demobilised servicemen objected to being called 'plotters' by a wealthy resident in the parish magazine because they had wanted a parish hall. The men contrasted this with their homecoming when they were called heroes and said the insult was an attempt to create strife and ill-feeling.[54] At a public meeting in Honiton the mayor chastised two men, one of whom was a local medical doctor and the other the rector, Reverend the Honourable F. L. Courtenay, who was the brother of the Earl of Devon, for their 'un-businesslike' manner in suggesting a site for the Memorial Hall. They said to him 'We have done our best and you seem to treat us, the Rector and I, as a pair of naughty boys. I have never heard anything so discourteous from a Chairman...' Amongst the subsequent discussion the mayor said 'you just mind what you are talking about, my boy, in a public meeting' and later 'you are not going to put me down. I am Chairman of this meeting and you are the Rector.'[55] There was also a full parish meeting called in Harberton over a dispute on whether the memorial tablet should be alabaster or marble. There had been a covert attempt to change a prior decision and villagers objected. Two resigned from the committee.[56]

Feelings were occasionally heated towards clerics. There were acrimonious feelings in Shaldon against the vicar or so he suggested. The Reverend Marsh-Dunn, presiding at a meeting of the committee, was disappointed his scheme had attracted little support. He noted there was 'manifest coldness' towards his church and asked the audience to reject the 'absurd idea' that the building was his own personal property.[57] What the cleric failed to say was that he had given the land on which the church was built, which would have accounted for enhancing the identification between him and it.[58] Perhaps more importantly, he failed to understand why people did not consider a new church roof the most appropriate way to commemorate the war dead. At Uplowman, near Tiverton, one resident complained with some vigour that the vicar had misinformed a previous public meeting by inflating the costs of a competing scheme in order that he could beautify his church with a stained glass window.[59]

Halberton may have heard the bitterest comments against a cleric. In January 1919 parishioners in this village near Tiverton were so enraged by their vicar that they petitioned the bishop. They objected to his notion that the most 'beautiful way' to honour the men was to convert a side chapel into a lady chapel. They claimed local people did not want it and petitioned that the vicar 'is anxious to have the same principally for his own benefit, the wishes of parishioners and relatives of the fallen being quite a secondary consideration'. The petitioners, who

15. *The clock-tower at Shaldon which was not the choice of the local Anglican cleric.*

included a churchwarden, explained that the vicar had raised funds for the chapel ahead of a public meeting and in which he suggested he had widespread support. The petitioners also noted that instead of a church embellishment they had decided to have a village hall.[60] The vicar wrote to the *Tiverton Gazette* to give his side, while writing that he had no intention of engaging in a newspaper controversy, and one parishioner supported his scheme.[61] However, within a few months some eight hundred pounds were raised for a hall and it opened shortly afterwards. Tiverton's mayor unveiled the hall and complimented the village on raising the funds. He said it was a challenge to Tiverton which was aiming to raise similar finances for a hall from a population ten times the size. The mayor also praised them for choosing a hall as a war memorial but neglected to mention the vicar.[62]

Comments were occasionally critical once designs were unveiled. At Exeter the city design was immediately and repeatedly criticised by readers of the *Devon & Exeter Gazette*. Some were derisory of the semi-nudity of the figures, one thought it was scandalous that an airman was not one of the figures, another wanted a 'less gaudy' design and yet one more suggested the city should merely have a replica of the Cenotaph. Another reader even thought it was an unfortunate copy of a German monument.[63] At Teignmouth one resident wrote to the local newspaper:

'There seems to be a great deal of controversy about the Teignmouth War Memorial. I see the committee has decided to erect an obelisk. In my opinion – which I believe is not by any means an isolated one – had they tried for a hundred years they could hardly have found anything uglier or more inappropriate. Surely the memory of the men who gave their lives for their country is worthy of something better than such an offence to the eyesight? The sight of it would be enough to cause another war'.[64]

One resident asked for her subscription money to be returned because she objected to the design.[65] The harshness of these criticisms was repeated across the county with perhaps the most bizarre criticism being levelled at the village of Ide. Its committee had to contend with interference in the design from the district council when one of its members suggested that without supervision Ide could erect a gibbet.[66]

Communities decided whose details were recorded. Many listed those who died but others also commemorated those who served. This was up to each community except if the monument was placed in an Anglican church. Early in 1920 the Bishop of Exeter instructed his churches that only those who died were to be recorded.[67] Littlehempston near Totnes was one of many parishes to have the dead recorded in the church and the survivors in the porch.[68] In some churches this separate list of those that served can still be found in the porch such as at Cruwys Morchard or Pilton near Barnstaple. That at Poughill is on the exterior wall above the door to the church. This presented unexpected problems: at Widecombe-In-The-Moor as early as October 1920 the hand-written roll of honour had decayed and there were complaints it was too dilapidated to serve its purpose.[69] Some rolls of service are also noted on lych-gates such as Widworthy and Ilsington. Over the following decades most, but not all, of these moved into the churches. Other denominations had no such rules. The Wesleyans and the Baptists erected memorials internally which listed both those that died and those that returned from the war. Some have a further category: these listed those who had been wounded. This was the case in Petrockstowe which noted men who had died, those who had served and 'these suffered hurt'. Many memorials did not because they were erected in 1919 and 1920 when some of the men were still dying. One such man who could have easily been ignored was Private Garfield Peardon of Buckfastleigh who died in an Edinburgh hospital early in 1919. He had been a prisoner of war and it was noted at his death 'he had been practically starved to death and never recovered from his experience'. Peardon was buried in Buckfastleigh[70] and had a claim to be a war casualty as much as those who had died overseas. Likewise in 1924 James Roberts was buried on the eve of the unveiling of the Plympton St Maurice war memorial. He was thirty years old and had not recovered from wounds he received in 1916.[71] At Kentisbeare the men are recorded collectively for their service and the tablet also names two men who were 'killed in action' and another five who 'died and buried hard by'.[72] Each community had to decide for itself who should be listed.

There are also differences between parishes over who was defined as a local man. Sandford listed men who joined locally as well as those who had near relations living in the parish. After they erected their memorial it was discovered that four men were omitted and the details of eight others were wrong. This included some serious errors: Charles Ball should have been George Ball and Harry Bowden should have been Horace Bowden but it was too costly to rectify. The committee did not take any responsibility but recorded in their records it was 'solely due to the apathy of relatives that these mistakes had occurred'.[73] At Parkham the men on the wall tablet had either lived or worked in the parish or their parents lived there. Some men are also listed on more than one Devon memorial because their parents resided in one parish but the men had been born in another.

In some places there was considerable discussion on what personal details to record. Bridestowe debated whether to place names alphabetically or by regiment; a parish meeting decided to list the men alphabetically despite letters from some relatives.[74] At Cofton near Dawlish the cross recorded the men by the year, month and day in which they died. The monument for Clyst Hydon listed the men by their seniority and noted not merely the day they died but also the location. For example, two of the men were listed as 'Lieutenant Corporal Norman Horsham died in Rouen Hospital April 22nd 1917' and 'Private

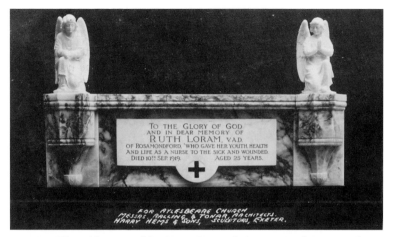

16. *The tablet erected by Harry Hems & Sons to Ruth Loram of Aylesbeare. The photograph was used by the firm.*

Harry Parsons, Devonshire Regiment, Killed at Ypres, May 9th 1915'.[75]

It would be natural to assume from reading the memorials that only men died in the war. Most community memorials refer to the loss of men but some monuments noted women as well. Sidmouth's tablet, for example, recorded the death of a V.A.D. nurse, Mary Gertrude Tindall,[76] while the tablet for South Brent noted it was 'to the honour and unfading memory of the men and women of this parish'.[77] On it was inscribed the names of Mary Rowlands (Queen Mary's Army Auxiliary Corps) and Margaret Carew (Voluntary Aid Detachments). Likewise, two women are recorded on the tablet for Bideford's Anglican church.[78] Northam's memorial records the death of Miss E. Stella Temple, Commandant of a Red Cross Convoy. That at Heavitree includes Annie Studley Broster who was listed in the parish official book as being a nurse who died of disease on March 27th 1916 aged 55.[79] Another is at Yarnscombe which lists all the parishioners by their surname and an initial for their first name, without any titles, except for 'Miss W. Down'.

There are also private tablets to women. At Halberton is one to Winifred English who died at the Red Cross hospital in Exeter while on duty in 1915. One of the main memorials to women was erected in 1919; that year a marble tablet was placed in Torquay's Municipal Buildings to note the work of the Red Cross and the V.A.D. nurses. Some 6,000 men had been treated by scores of nurses.[80] It is difficult to know how widespread was the view expressed by one letter-writer to Exeter's *Express & Echo* who criticised the city's monument in the context of the struggle for women to have the vote which, it would appear, he felt had been lost. He regarded the design as expressive of female emancipation: in the monument he saw St George as having been usurped by a woman disguised as Victory and felt the figure of a nurse should be more cheerful and have her nursing gear replaced by a typewriter.[81]

Clerics also served overseas, such as those from Topsham and Chagford,[82] and at least one Anglican vicar, Reverend F. W. Hewitt of Brixton near Plymouth, died in the war. He was killed whilst 'ministering to the wounded at the Battle of Loos'. A Wesleyan minister at Exeter also died whilst serving: Reverend Clifford Reed was twenty-eight years old when he died on Messines Ridge in 1917. Those that remained at home were, in some cases, influenced by patriotism and expressed this at unveilings. For instance, it was far from a Christian attitude that the vicar of Berry Pomeroy articulated when he said Germans were incapable of understanding human nature and ideals.[83]

## Sites

One difficulty was the question of where to place memorials. This was problematic given the number of existing memorials. It would have been impossible for the people of Buckland Monachorum to have erected a cross in the Anglican churchyard given there was already there a towering cross to commemorate Queen Victoria. Other Anglican churches,

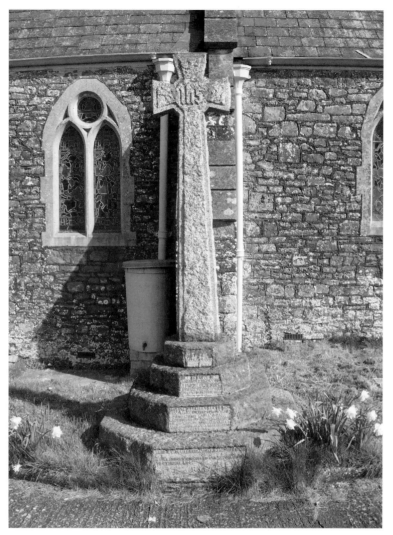

17. *Memorial cross at Butterleigh erected to the memory of Alfred Lewis Noon, son of the rector, who died at the age of twenty.*

like that at Ivybridge, also had private memorial crosses to individuals who died in the Great War. That particular one could easily be confused for a community cross. In both of these cases it would have been sensible to erect new crosses elsewhere. Likewise, at Butterleigh the rector erected his own cross to the memory of his twenty-two year old son who was killed in France. It would have been an expensive endeavour to have erected a more imposing cross than the private one already in place in Modbury's Anglican churchyard which may explain why an obelisk was sited elsewhere.

The cost of land was also a consideration. At Pinhoe the committee attempted to buy land from Lord Poltimore but they felt his price was too high. They were forced to use the Anglican churchyard.[84] Many sites were given which formed part of large estates. That for Sidbury's cross was a gift of Sir Charles Cave of Sidbury Manor, the large landowner in the parish. The Cave family was overwhelmingly concerned with the monument: it was unveiled by Mrs Cave and designed by Walter Cave, a London architect who obviously was related to the family.[85] Likewise at Ashprington a major landowner provided the site for the memorial[86] and similar land was given in Kingskerswell amongst other places.[87] A striking example is Combe Martin where land was given by the three Misses Toms, the daughters of the late rector. It was the only freehold land they owned in the town.[88] A different type of gift was made at Bishopsteignton: the cross is positioned near the Wesleyan chapel because the Nonconformists gave the site.[89] Other monuments were erected in local cemeteries such as at Great Torrington and South Molton.

Urban memorials were usually on land assigned by local government. One of the most protracted disputes took place in Ilfracombe. One newspaper called it 'very regrettable' and 'unseemly'. The objections began in 1919 and these caused the monument not to be erected for five years. It was almost the last of Devon's town memorials. One early argument was that a position where holiday makers promenaded would detract from a memorial's dignity and four years later no less than 160 ratepayers successfully petitioned Ilfracombe Urban District Council not to permit the memorial on the Parade. Other delays were due to disagreement over which type of memorial to erect and over the financing for what proved to be an unsuccessful scheme.[90] Eventually it was placed within a specially created Garden of Remembrance near the main Anglican church but away from the busier and noisier seafront.

This question of location dogged committees. Dawlish was typical. Eleven former military men suggested the memorial would be isolated if situated between thatched cottages and the churchyard. The church's distance from the seafront was a contributing factor. The men wrote that it was commonly being asked in the resort 'why don't the committee have it fixed in a prominent place, the same as other towns are doing?' A meeting was held for friends and family of the dead men and they chose outside the church rather than in York Gardens. At one public meeting it was suggested the churchyard was more reverential than a position in the public gardens given the scenes of 'joyous gaiety' in the summer season.[91]

Devonport did not want a site which was one of quiet contemplation but the chairman of the committee said they wanted one which was 'in our midst easily accessible'. Moreover, the committee chose the public park so that it was visible to the Keyham dockyard and to all ships entering and leaving the port. Its great height helped its visibility. This may have been due more to civic pride than to any other consideration.[92]

There were hesitations about giving money in Honiton until it was determined where the Memorial Hall would be sited. There were comments at a meeting at the Dolphin Hotel that the price asked for land was exorbitant and that it was 'a rotten place'. The mayor openly said that he hoped the rector would be liberal in giving a site.[93] Within six months

18. *Combe Martin's monument, placed within a discreet area in front of the parish church.*

19. *Salcombe's memorial, prominently situated in front of the town hall and with an inspiring view of the estuary.*

20. *Honiton's monument placed in the centre of the town.*

21. *Hemyock's Great War cross was situated near the Anglican church but in the centre of the village.*

22. *Bovey Tracey had its war memorial cross placed near the town hall along the High Street.*

23. *Seaton's Cross, placed within the secluded*
*Anglican churchyard.*

24. *Ivybridge's cross was placed at a distance from the Anglican church and in the centre.*

25. *East Down's memorial was erected*
*in front of the Anglican church.*

26. *The town cemetery is the location
for Great Torrington's memorial.*

27. *Sidmouth's memorial was not placed near the seafront but within the Anglican churchyard.*

28. *Stoke Fleming's restored cross was erected
in front of the parish church.*

29. *Witheridge had its war memorial cross placed within the parish churchyard.*

30. *Sowton's unusual memorial is at a
distance from the Anglican church.*

*31. Buckland Monachorum's cross is situated in open moorland.*

*32. Stoke Gabriel's design must have adapted to the unusual position. It was unveiled in November 1920 and designed by T. N. Dinwiddy. The cross was carved of Dartmoor granite and cost £232.*

*33. An open position in Morchard Bishop at the heart of the village.*

the entire scheme was abandoned because local people refused to support the building in that location.[94]

The positions found at Ilfracombe and Dawlish is similar to the sites decided at Barnstaple, Bideford, Combe Martin, Dartmouth, Seaton and Sidmouth as well as at Exeter and Plymouth. Other seaside resorts erected their monuments within the main promenades such as Budleigh Salterton, Kingsbridge, Teignmouth and Torquay. Exmouth's memorial was not placed along the seafront but in the busy main square as was that at Paignton. Lynton's monument was also situated in the main street. Inland towns had a similar pattern. Those at Cullompton, Holsworthy, Okehampton and South Molton were placed in quiet situations while others, such as Ashburton, Crediton, Honiton, Ivybridge, Newton Abbot, Tavistock and Totnes were prominently sited in main thoroughfares. Some chose a site for dignity and quiet contemplation while others wanted the monument to be as conspicuous as possible.

Committees also disagreed on how to position the memorial. At Salcombe Regis there were two views: should the cross be best positioned for visitors to see it as they approached from Sidmouth or should the cross be 'sentimentally' placed looking towards the village and church?[95] They opted for the cross to face the road. The name of its location alone was highly appropriate: it was positioned on Soldiers' Hill.

## Religious divisions

In many places there were separate wall tablets for the Anglicans and for other groups within their own buildings. The Jewish synagogue, for example, has its own memorial in Plymouth. Community memorials generally listed all denominations but occasionally there were disagreements between religious groups. In 1919 a parish meeting was held in Bittaford to canvass opinion on the type of memorial and shortly afterwards it was agreed to erect tablets in all places of worship. There was upset when it later transpired that funds which had been raised for the tablet in the Wesleyan chapel were instead to be spent only on one for the Anglican church. Shortly afterwards a protest meeting was held[96] but the parish memorial became a cross situated in front of the parish church. A meeting at Willand considered a request from the Wesleyans to contribute to their own roll of honour. One of those who attended objected to the proposed memorial and said 'they should have something more substantial than a parchment roll of honour. They are part of the parish as well as our lads and I think their lads deserve something a little better than is suggested'.[97] Barnstaple was like many other places in that voices were raised that the public monument should not be sited in one religious building as would then restrict it to one particular denomination.[98] At Drewsteignton the rector suggested at the public meeting that the war memorial should be a screen in his church but there were objections that the parish needed a monument which included Nonconformists.

Cooperation between religious groups was expected and was often achieved when the communal memorials were unveiled. In some places they worked well together such as during the dedication service at the Anglican church at Buck's Cross near Bideford when the chapel was closed in order for everyone to collectively honour the dead.[99] The dedication ceremony for Chulmleigh's great cross was typical in that it involved Anglican, Methodist and Congregational clerics.[100] The pastor of the Dalwood United Methodist Chapel told his audience at the unveiling of their tablet that he felt the occasion was part of the recent service held at the Anglican church in which two other memorials were unveiled to honour local men. He was assisted in his event by the Anglican vicar.[101] Across Devon many parishes managed to come together, if only briefly, to honour their dead.

Separate parishes even cooperated. The two parishes of East and West Worlington erected a joint war memorial cross at a site between the two villages[102] and in 1920 when three parishes in north-western Dartmoor joined together to erect

34. *The unveiling of Chulmleigh's Great War cross, 1920. It was described at the time as of 'Coker design' with a finial and five crosses in one. It was carved by J. T. Miller of Okehampton.*

a single monument. In May that year a collection of Anglican and Methodist clergy processed to the meeting point of Lew Trenchard, Marystowe and Thrushelton. On the village green of Lewdown they were joined by schoolchildren and ex-servicemen who watched the unveiling of the memorial. The lead cleric was the writer Reverend Sabine Baring-Gould. Unlike any other Devon memorial this one lists the men in three separate categories of resident parish.[103] In the largest urban areas, at Plymouth and Exeter, the community memorials were generally restricted to interior tablets and not to creating outside monuments because local support was given to a large civic monument.

## Financing

Committees handled most of the financial arrangements including the most daunting task of raising funds. Colyton agreed to have two memorials, a cross and Institute, so the members needed to find £1,700. The members explained afterwards that they sent a 'hat' around the village and instantly raised £550. The remaining funds were raised through other donations, whist drives, dances and a country fair.[104] Other places had similar efforts. The papers of the war memorial committee at Sandford show how individuals canvassed the parish and brought in varying sums, some as low as only a few pennies. Comparable accounts for Brampford Speke near Exeter show similar amounts were raised there.[105]

In many places contributions were sought by canvassing every household but in Barnstaple the mayor was against this; his view was that donations should be given spontaneously and that soliciting funds was unseemly.[106] He would have been unhappy to hear about fundraising at Plympton St Maurice: they laid a 'mile of pennies' to raise money.[107] In some places there was no need: at East Budleigh the village tablet was paid for by an anonymous parishioner.[108] Likewise, at Starcross a local woman paid for a parish tablet and a cleric paid for

Dear Sir or Madam,—

## PARISH OF CHURSTON FERRERS

## WAR MEMORIAL.

A Committee was formed at a Public Meeting held on the 8th inst. for the purpose of raising a Memorial to those of this Parish who have fallen in the War, and they suggested the design of a Cross of about 9—11 feet as being the most appropriate.

They were also authorised to collect Subscriptions and to report to a subsequent Meeting.

It was also suggested that the site of the Memorial should be on the Warborough Common.

I shall be glad to know whether you approve of these suggestions, and also to know whether you will subscribe to this object.

The Committee feel that in order to make the Memorial as representative as possible, subscriptions, however small, will be gratefully received.

Kindly let me have your reply on or before the 30th March.

Yours truly,

HAYNE SMITH,

*Hon. Sec. and Treas.*

35. *Fundraising effort of the committee at Churston Ferrers.*

two priests' stalls to honour his nephew who had died in the war.[109] This was not the case in South Brent where the War Memorial Committee investigated whether it was possible to have their memorial paid for by increasing local rates. Perhaps not surprisingly there were objections.[110]

Kingsbridge was one of Devon's towns which found it difficult to raise funds. It had a generation of failure in finding money for other schemes and the war memorial campaign was similarly blighted. The honorary secretary tried to rally the town with a speech when the plans were unveiled. Mr Stoneman reminded them of the past failures and added:

'Never in the history of the world was there a time when the people should show their thankfulness as at the present time, and in no part of their beautiful country was there greater reason for thankfulness than in lovely Devon where they had hardly known there was a war on.'

He conceded that working class men and women could not give much but hoped that they would all contribute and proposed that working men gave one day's wages every three months. Stoneman added that wealthier people should give more and he suggested that money left in accounts for previous schemes should be donated to the war memorial cause. When the monument was unveiled, six years later when every other Devon town had erected their memorial, it was admitted that during those intervening years the committee had 'experienced difficulties which appeared almost insurmountable'.[111] The result was, however, a monument unique in Devon.

In 1919 the committee at Paignton did what seemed like good business practice by considering two tenders. They were most likely being sensitive to hiring local firms, given the economic uncertainty at the time, and asked two local firms for estimates of their costs. The people of Paignton had not given sufficient money to erect a monument equal to the committee's aspirations so costs were important as a consideration. It must have galled the committee that Torquay was able to raise money more easily and that it subsequently had a much grander memorial which was by one of the leading designers of the time.[112]

## Two tenders for war memorials at Paignton, 1919[113]

| Mr J. Pollard of Paignton | | Messrs Jenkins of Torquay |
|---|---|---|
| 15 feet | £186 | £174 10s |
| 16 feet | £195 | £207 10s |
| 17 feet | £205 | £256 15s |
| 18 feet | £220 | £307 |
| 19 feet | £234 | £356 |

Across the county other committees compared similar estimates to establish the best value. Cost became of great concern to Paignton which found it was unable to raise amounts comparable to other places. Oddly enough, Herbert Read advised one committee not to seek a great number of estimates. He told them the lowest one usually withdrew his offer once he discovered 'that Dick, Tom and Harry' were much higher. His advice was to 'choose a good man you could trust'.[114]

# THREE

# THE CHOICES IN A MEMORIAL

Choosing the type of monument was the most contentious issue facing committees. For private individuals it was generally straightforward. Some chose crosses but the majority of individuals elected to erect wall tablets that were placed in houses of worship. Because of the cost these were limited to those who had sufficient disposable funds. They were easier to erect partly because fewer people were involved in making decisions. These were generally wall tablets, made of stone or metal, and were placed in churches or chapels. An unusual one was that to Captain Nigel Hunter on the western slopes of Dartmoor: it was imbedded in the landscape. The tablet, along with a seat, was erected at Black Rock because the deceased had visited it, a favourite place, just before he left for the Western Front. It includes lines of poetry he had written as verses of farewell.[115]

Hundreds of these personal tablets were erected in Devon to mark the deaths of particular individuals. Occasionally private individuals even paid for the community church tablets which recorded all the parishioners or members of the congregation. This happened at Marldon as well as at Buckerell.[116] At St Thomas near Exeter the parents of two brothers who died

36. *The war memorial committee at Exwick.*

in France paid for the tablets for all the parishioners. Some
were erected not by family or friends but by others with more
unusual connections. At East Teignmouth's Anglican church
can be seen a memorial to Seaman William Broom, a twenty-
six year old, who drowned on the *Thamesmaid* whilst serving
his country. The tablet was erected by his former employer
who was the owner of a Teignmouth-built yacht, the *Anita*.[117]
As with crosses, Devon's craftsmen provided memorial tablets
for buildings across the county. Harry Hems & Sons of Exeter
were typical in that they executed work not only in and around
Exeter but across Devon and throughout the country.[118]

Other wall tablets were raised by the community and these
could be of wood, stone or metal. One of the most striking
and unusual tablets was created by Harry Hems & Sons
for Roseash Church. It was carved of alabaster and features
a standing soldier in khaki kit.[119] It is similar to that at
Abbotskerswell which has both a sailor and soldier.

Those that collectively represented service and sacrifice proved more awkward to reach a consensus. Every community was tested in their decisions. Some community memorials were modest such as that at Denbury which took the shape of a tablet fixed to the existing fountain in the square.[120] Musbury has another unassuming monument: it erected a simple stone tablet at the entrance to the church.[121]

The committees had to decide between a beneficial or ornamental monument. Should it be a memorial that benefited communities in meaningful ways or should they be artistic expressions? Barnstaple was typical of the contrasting opinions heard in public meetings. A number of proposals were made in 1919 including that St Anne's Chapel should be turned into a war museum, several ladies wanted a crucifix placed outside that chapel and others suggested money should be raised for an isolation hospital, a district nurse, the provision of a bathing place, a club or a meeting place for soldiers.[122] The opening up of meetings to public suggestions produced a surprising range of ideas across Devon. At Budleigh Salterton local residents not only suggested a clock tower, servicemen's club and a shrine but also a cairn on West Down Beacon.[123] Budleigh Salterton was not alone in its range of ideas: Torquay also had a varied list of suggested monuments that year. In February 1919 the mayor reported that wishes had been expressed for a shrine, obelisk or other monument in Princess Gardens, Corbyn's Head or Babbacombe Down and another suggestion was one hundred houses should be built for working men. One local thought the new YMCA building should be the resort's war memorial and another wanted an art museum and gallery. Another proposal was to provide a grand organ for the town hall.[124] Totnes had similar discussions with one idea being that a playing field should be acquired for local children. The town sought to lease the Castle from the Duke of Somerset but the duke responded 'I prefer keeping it in my own hands at present'. The mayor said that they 'ought to try to do something to make the lives of the children and young people and their poorer neighbours

37–40. *Two wall tablets for Tamerton Foliot and Abbotsham and St Giles in-the-Heath.*

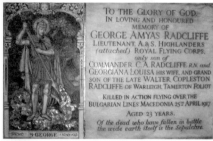

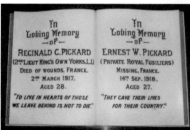

41–44. *Wall tablets for Dalwood, Shobrooke, St Giles-in-the Wood and Yarcombe.*

45–48. *Wall tablets for Fremington, Chudleigh Knighton, Beer and Shillingford.*

of a recreation ground but also of a public hall, a school, museum or public library. The people of Totnes were reminded that 750 local men had gone to war and that 100 of them had not returned. An appropriate memorial was, they were told, necessary to show their appreciation for the men's service and sacrifices.[125] Another town which had many suggestions was Newton Abbot. One man suggested the purchase of Forde, the large historic house located at the edge of the town and which has since become the headquarters of Teignbridge District Council. He said it would become a white elephant but that would be better than 'erecting a slab of granite'. Other ideas were swimming baths, scholarships for orphans, a fountain, an 'artistic' memorial in Courtenay Park, and an almshouse for soldiers' widows.[126] Cullompton also discussed ideas which were termed white elephants such as drinking fountains, lamp posts, clock towers and bandstands which led one writer to suggest that cottages could be built instead.[127] One proposal for Teignmouth was a pond in the Den but it was pointed out that there was sufficient water already along the seafront.[128] At Bampton one local advocated a children's park[129] and at Sampford Peverell among ten suggestions was the providing of electricity to the village as a memorial.[130] Stoke Gabriel discussed a public telephone.[131] Bradninch had a long list of suggestions including a recreation ground, bandstand and ambulance. The winning proposal at that meeting was a swimming bath.[132] In nearly every village, town and city suggestions poured in as to what was considered the most appropriate form a memorial could take. Committees were faced with trying to negotiate varying expectations and desires.

Some communities could not decide upon one single memorial and instead voted for a range of monuments. Dartmouth was one. In 1919 the port's committee decided to pursue erecting public baths, washhouses and drying rooms as well as a shelter on the front and a triumphal arch in New Ground Gardens.[133] Others chose a particular freestanding monument but eventually learned that there was insufficient support. Brixham was one of these. It considered a public park, a granite column and a clock tower. It decided upon the latter but eventually erected a cross.[134] Many parishes had schemes which did not work. Some were too costly, like the memorial hall at Honiton, while others, such as a wooden tablet intended for Lympstone church, were more modest but still failed.[135] Paignton could not raise the finances for the scheme they had commissioned from Mr A. G. Wallis and opted instead for a cheaper granite obelisk.[136] At Heavitree outside Exeter the proposed cross was abandoned after insufficient funds were raised. Instead they placed a tablet in the church.[137]

In some communities the committees opted for a poll in order that residents could decide. In the village of Shaldon, across the river Teign from Teignmouth, members of the public were given five options: they could vote for working with Teignmouth to improve hospital facilities, a public clock, providing a parish nurse, a new roof for the church or erecting a public shelter. The residents voted for the clock and decided that any extra money raised would support a memorial cross in the ancillary community of Ringmore or a tablet in the parish church.[138] Votes were also held in Exmouth because of a general uncertainty as to what the town wanted. A poorly-attended public meeting in the summer of 1919 had previously voted for a non-religious monument but the Chairman, upon being urged by some residents who were not at the meeting to reconsider that decision, held a second public meeting which decided upon a public ballot. Perhaps not surprisingly, local churchmen wanted the first decision overturned. No less than 6,080 postal ballots were sent out but only half were returned. Of them 55 per cent voted for a cross and 44 per cent wanted a non-religious monument. The return showed, according to one journalist, a 'lamentable lack of interest'.[139] Other decisions were made exclusively within committees: at Lynton the council informed a public meeting that it had decided the town's memorial would be a monument outside the town hall.[140]

Temporary memorials were erected partly to give local people the opportunity to see what the proposed monument would look like. This was the case with Lutyen's cross which was first constructed of wood and placed in its preferred site near the West Front of Exeter's Cathedral. Likewise, Exmouth situated a wooden model in the Strand.[141] What was described as a Cenotaph was erected at the Three Cornered Plot in Sidmouth in 1920. It bore no relation to the Cenotaph in London: that at Sidmouth was a tall column surmounted by an ornate cap.[142] Paignton also had what was called a Cenotaph; this was a temporary wooden one set up the year before in Palace Avenue. There was also a cross at the seafront. The two structures were built for an outdoor memorial service in the summer of 1919.[143] Also that year, before Torquay had its permanent memorial there was a makeshift one, termed a war shrine, set up on the Strand for Peace Day in July 1919. It was bedecked with flowers and flags and had at least three crosses. There were others throughout the borough[144] but earlier that year one Torquinian deplored the state of shrines with their dead flowers and dirty vases.[145] Although these were erected as temporary structures they helped inform the public in later deciding what type of permanent memorial should be created. In Paignton the appearance of its temporary monument made local people say with what was said to have been one voice, and with a great din, 'here is what we want in stone or granite and on this spot'.[146]

Arguments for a memorial of practical use, those that would make a useful contribution to society, were voiced by many people, particularly by those who had fought in the war. They contended that cold stone would not honour those who died nor benefit those whose lives had been fractured by the war. Early in 1919 a plea was made by a resident of the north Devon village of Bishop's Nympton that the type of memorial should be carefully considered. It was his opinion that decisions were made rashly without thinking of the long-term consequences. He conceded that stone memorials were the most popular but questioned whether they quickly were forgotten and overlooked. He thought that six months later the village pump would generate more interest. Interestingly, he argued that not only did such memorials not bring comfort to the bereaved but that they were a constant reminder of the horrors and sufferings that were endured. They would be, he wrote, 'a monument over the grave of the lost hopes of a revivified village life.' He suggested community halls were the key to rebuilding village life and that they would encourage social harmony: he thought that only in a village hall could Non-conformists and Anglicans meet and that it was only there that 'social distinctions might disintegrate'.[147] In contrast, a discharged soldier in Dartmouth told an open meeting to leave public utility schemes to local authorities and give the ex-servicemen what they wanted, which were stone monuments.[148] The division between the two views was forcibly brought out in a public meeting at Hartland in 1919. The rector suggested a monument was appropriate and added he 'did not think anything that ministered to the pleasure, comfort or use of the living would be an appropriate memorial to those that had laid down their lives for us'. It was reported that another speaker protested 'violently'. He said 'such a monument would mean cruelty to the friends of the fallen by reminding them of their loss every time they passed. He was sure if the lads could tell us their own wishes they would be that something should be done for the comfort of their fellows that had come back. He suggested nothing could be better than an Institute or Recreation Ground'.[149]

It would simplistic to argue there was a division between the wealthy who wanted ornamental monuments and the poorer who had a need for schemes that would improve their lives. Even so, as will be discussed in the following pages, the county's Lord Lieutenant, Earl Fortescue, saw no reason for the County of Devon to erect what he dismissed as schemes of public utility. He had earlier advocated erecting a monument surmounted by captured German guns, an idea which the Dean of Exeter must have been at pains to accommodate at the cathedral and would have been difficult for many to have envisioned as ornamental. When Fortescue chose the steering committee for deciding the form of the memorial he excluded those who had wanted functional memorials. This left a collection of members of the upper classes who faithfully served and duly erected a stone cross in Cathedral Yard at Exeter. What they thought of Washfield's aforementioned public shelter in the village green is not known. It is unlikely that they would have approved of one man's suggestion for a memorial in Paignton which would be both useful as well as ornamental: he proposed, probably not in a jocular way, a 'horse drawn or motor driven road sweeping brush'.[150]

# FOUR

# BENEFICIAL MONUMENTS

The type of monument which was intended to enhance lives were variously praised or derided as being utilitarian, useful, practical, functional or beneficial. Deliberations at Ilfracombe show how strongly public support could be. In 1919 a public meeting heard calls for purchasing an x-ray machine for the cottage hospital, building an almshouse or maternity centre, and creating a recreation ground. One of the resort's clerics suggested an inexpensive cross and a gymnasium while another supported not just a library but the implementation of six-hour working days. The latter thought that erecting a freestanding monument was like offering a stone to children who were asking for bread.[151] There were few calls then in the town for a memorial cross or obelisk.

Irrespective of some determined opposition to them many communities across Devon successfully erected these memorials and the vast majority still serve their original function nearly a century later. The most common scheme was a village hall. Dozens were built throughout Devon. Some were Memorial Halls and others Victory Halls.[152] Kenn simply named its war memorial 'Kenn Parish Hall'.[153] Some parishes joined forces for a hall: this happened in May 1920 when the foundation

*49. The dignitaries laying the foundation stone for
Northlew and Ashbury village hall.*

stone was laid by Field Marshal Lord Methuen for the Victory
Hall built for the parishes of Northlew and Ashbury.[154] It
opened less than a year later and had been built partly with
stone given by local men.[155] The need for a hall in Lapford
had been recognised before the war and at the signing of the
Peace Truce plans began to build a Victory Hall.[156] Even so,
a Braunton man suggested to Exeter in 1919 that the erection
of village halls was self-indulgence with an excuse. He argued
that there was no need for them before the war and that a
poorer country could not afford them afterwards.[157] Despite
his claims the halls were tremendously popular.

There were also many calls in Paignton for a memorial hall
but the resort ended up with an obelisk. The proposal for a
hall was condemned by some as utilitarian and the *Paignton
Observer* noted in an editorial that:

'the obvious retort is that utility, combined with worthy commemorative features, is what should be aimed at on the grounds of true economy and the benefit of those for whom the departed died. We have nothing to say against putting up a sacred emblem by those who are prepared to subscribe privately to it, but it is felt by a very large number that such is not a desirable town memorial, especially under the circumstances of the great need for an assembly hall in the town.'[158]

The low amount of money subsequently raised from the public may reflect dissatisfaction with the committee's choice. Certainly one resident wrote that he would not contribute to a clock tower or 'any other showy but useless thing'. A memorial hall was most commonly suggested but the committee failed to support it.[159] One likely factor was that its near rival, Torquay, was erecting an impressive monument by one of the country's most prestigious designers, Sir Reginald Blomfield.

There was also disappointment in Slapton where ex-servicemen tried to erect a hall when they came back from the war. The men each contributed some of the pay they received when they returned but discovered they had insufficient support in the village particularly among some older residents who felt they would not personally benefit from a village hall. The idea then fermented for several years and in 1925 a building was finally erected.[160]

The hall at Broadhembury had a difficult course. In 1919 Mrs Rose Gundry of The Grange conceived of the idea of a Memorial Hall and it opened a year later but only after a great deal of heart ache and sour village politics. Cedric Drewe, who was chairman of the parish council and whose family had formerly lived at The Grange, opposed the scheme. Mrs Gundry offered in October 1919 to provide the site, building materials and a large donation towards the other costs. A Vestry Meeting supported her. Six months later, in March, Drewe chaired a parish meeting which decided on cost grounds not to proceed with the scheme but to have instead a cross which he

81

later provided a site for. The vicar explained this in the parish magazine and was at pains to state that the village should remember how indebted they were to Drewe for his providing the current reading room. Mrs Gundry was obviously not one to be put off. A month later she held a meeting in the village at which Sir John Green, of the Ministry of Agriculture, and Nugent Harris, Organiser for the Village Clubs Association, convinced the audience to restart the scheme. A few months later Mrs Gundry announced she had obtained a considerable grant, of two hundred pounds, from the Rural League. Mrs Gundry's hall opened that October and Drewe's cross was unveiled the following summer. Interestingly, the grant may have been influenced by the fact that the mother of the Right Hon. Jesse Collings, who was influential in the League, had lived in Broadhembury.[161] Broadhembury illustrates another influencing factor in the hall schemes: rural regeneration was an issue with other bodies such as the Carnegie Trust.

Other hall schemes failed such as at Axminster and Ashburton where there were insufficient funds.[162] Honiton had the same history. In some places considerable financial help should have made it relatively easy for plans to succeed. At Beer Lord Clinton provided a site for a war memorial club and institute and an architect offered to oversee the work without charge.[163]

Whereas many clerics oversaw monuments and improvements destined for their churches the new rector of Diptford near Totnes was responsible for erecting a hall. Within fifteen months of the idea being mooted the village's new hall opened. The rector, described as a 'go-ahead gentleman', was told at the unveiling that they had achieved something villages ten times their size had been unable to do.[164]

Some halls were not new buildings. That at Belstone was an army hut. The residents of this Dartmoor parish near Okehampton heard at the dedication that no other building was more appropriate given that those who died had each spent time in a similar hut which had provided 'comparative

50. *The Tiverton war memorial, an extraordinarily ambitious scheme.*

peace and comfort'.[165] Colyton not only erected a cross but purchased an existing building, the Drill Hall. It was renamed the Memorial Institute.[166] One of the most ambitious schemes was successfully executed at Tiverton and this also used an existing building. Tiverton decided to purchase the Angel Hotel as a war memorial and it opened in about 1929.[167]

The second other most popular option for a public benefit monument was a public recreation ground. Devon had several parks and recreation grounds which became war memorials and dozens of others were suggested.[168] Although they were commonly suggested the finances were often beyond the reach of smaller communities such as Pinhoe near Exeter.[169] Totnes hoped the Duke of Somerset would provide the Castle for a recreation ground and at Bradninch it was suggested the Prince of Wales might provide some land.[170] Both places would be disappointed. At Buckland Monachorum one speaker at a public meeting suggested asking the lord of the manor and the Roborough Commoners for twenty acres to be laid out as the Victory Park but others at the meeting suggested local people preferred to walk openly in the moor rather than in a park.[171] Ilfracombe went to great lengths to acquire a field for a recreation ground. The committee adopted the idea but the local council decided the costs were too high: one field, it was said, would cost £18,000, a considerable sum at the time. At a public meeting one resident complained that all the existing recreation grounds catered for old men. Another man, who said he spoke as 'one of the boys that crawled back', noted that 'Waterloo was won on the playing fields of Eton'. Although there was great support for the idea the memorial in the resort became a column.[172]

However, at North Tawton three acres of land were given by Frank Gibbings, a former resident, as a recreation ground. He also pulled down eight derelict cottages to improve the situation, widened the road and left two hundred pounds to the town for a stone monument. The memorial still stands but the park has since been converted for use as the town cemetery.[173] A public recreation ground was also provided at Uffculme in East Devon. Two thousand pounds were raised in the village and amongst the facilities were two tennis courts, five bowling greens, a quoit pitch, pavilion and shelter.[174] Mount Pleasant in Clovelly was given by Mrs Hamlyn of Clovelly Court as a public recreation ground to the National Trust: it was intended by her to be a permanent memorial to the war.

Bideford had a bold plan: it decided to purchase Chudleigh Fort, a seventeenth-century site of some size across the river Torridge at East the Water, as a public amenity.[175] The nascent Labour party in Bideford objected to buying it on the grounds of hidden costs: they pointed out that several other schemes had been turned down on financial grounds[176] but the scheme went ahead and the park was opened in August 1921. No less than £1,250 had been raised by the public for the park.

A former mayor said at the unveiling that he had bid farewell at the railway station to most of the Bideford men who had served in the war and that he hoped that never again would local men be called upon to fight abroad.[177]

The town of Kingsbridge had been attempting to acquire a recreation ground for more than a generation but had been thwarted by insincere promises and by landowners who had blocked the acquisition of land. Finally, in 1919 Salt Mill Quay, a large plot of land near the promenade, was given to the town by the family of a former chairman of the urban council. The war memorial committee was then able to buy an adjoining lot of land and this was opened as a recreation ground. It took six years before this was supplemented by a stone monument.[178]

Crediton had probably the most difficult history of attempting a war memorial recreation ground: its actions resulted in a government enquiry. In May 1919 a Local Government Board Inspector examined witnesses into the local council's attempt to seek a loan of £1,400 to purchase a local field as a recreation ground and war memorial. He was told by a former chairman of the council that they had applied for a loan from the government but had been turned down. They then sought a private loan for the seven acres of pasture land which was needed to provide exercise for poor local children. It was argued that the only opposition came from wealthier residents of the town who objected to contributing to the costs. The inspector ruled against the council and early in 1920 the plans were dropped[179] but Newcombe's Meadow was later successfully acquired and still operates as a recreation ground.

Perhaps the most progressive of all the functional monuments were two hospitals, the Victory Wing to the Devon & Exeter Hospital and the Okehampton & District Cottage Hospital. The Exeter hospital, located in Southernhay, erected a Victory Wing in June 1922. Plans had been laid down three years before but it took that time to raise the £35,000 needed for the extension facing Magdalen Street. Half of the one hundred new beds were reserved for discharged soldiers. Amongst the modern innovations were rounded corners which did not allow dust to settle. The foundation stone was laid in January 1920 and the wing was opened two and half years later by Viscount Hambledon.[180] A few years later a similar effort took place in Okehampton: the foundation stone was laid in 1925 and it opened a year later in October 1926. Ex-servicemen raised most of the £6,700 for the building although the site was given by the former mayor. The men had first proposed a hospital as a war memorial in 1921 partly because of the lengthy waiting lists for the hospitals in Exeter and Plymouth.[181] Both buildings are now being redeveloped.

One of the most interesting of the practical monuments was made at Brixton. Two cottages were built to honour the memories of Lieut. Colonel Alfred Sunderland and Captain C. J. Spencer. Both men had died in France. It had been planned to build the two cottages near the Lafone Cottages at Pinhoe near Exeter but land was too costly. The houses were built with funds principally from Spencer's family, a friend of Sunderland's and the Mayoress of Exeter's Prisoner of War Fund. The buildings were intended to provide rent-free accommodation for men from the Devonshire Regiment.[182] They continued in the care of the Devonshire Regiment until relatively recently. Many other places discussed cottages for ex-servicemen, including Torquay,[183] but Brixton achieved it.

# FIVE

# ORNAMENTAL MONUMENTS

Ornamental or decorative memorials were the most prevalent as well as prominent war monuments and the vast majority of them were religious items. They generally took the form of embellishments to a church or chapel or as a freestanding cross which was placed in the landscape. Nearly all of Devon's ornamental memorials are of a conservative design which is both sombre and respectful. This is because the vast majority were erected in small villages and these decorative memorials were generally crosses, columns or obelisks. Only in larger urban areas were more creative memorials erected. Exeter, as the capital of the county, had the Devon County monumental as well as the Devonshire Regimental memorial and of course its own City monument. The county's other city, Plymouth, had in contrast the Royal Naval monument, the Royal Marines' memorial and its City monument. All of Devon's towns erected ornamental memorials and the majority of them had crosses including Barnstaple, Bideford, Brixham, Budleigh Salterton, Combe Martin, Dartmouth, Exmouth, Great Torrington, Holsworthy, Honiton, Ivybridge, Salcombe, Seaton, Sidmouth, South Molton, Tavistock and Totnes whereas only a few erected more unusual monuments such as Axminster, Ilfracombe, Lynton, Newton Abbot, Paignton, Plympton St Maurice, Teignmouth and Torquay.

## Crosses in the landscape

Crosses are Devon's most familiar war memorial because they appear most frequently as village monuments. More than 250 were erected throughout Devon and were created in places such as Welcombe in North Devon where few men died in the war.[184] Crosses were used as war memorials because they were seen by some as the ideal symbol of the war. The Dean of Exeter expressed this when he said, during the dedication of the cross at Whimple, that the two keynotes in Christ's life were the same as that of a soldier: service and sacrifice.[185] The cross was seen as a perpetual reminder of the relationship between the two: just as Christ had willingly died in service for mankind so too had Devon's servicemen given their lives

51. *The Great War cross at Branscombe which sits easily in the landscape.*

for the greater good. Moreover, the crosses reaffirmed the Christian belief about life after death. In 1919 the Bishop of Exeter told an audience gathered for the unveiling of one memorial cross that they:

'had done well in selecting for their war memorial the symbol of their faith. They could not honour those whose names were inscribed thereon more than by this choice of a memorial cross. Those whom they had loved – where were they? What had befallen them? Their bodies, they knew, lay in the dust of Flanders and foreign parts; but where were they? They were under the shadow of the cross, in the gracious keeping of the Crucified.'[186]

Crosses were, in effect, used as a symbol not just of sacrifice but of triumph.

In a handful of parishes ancient crosses were reused including at Cheriton Bishop, Torbryan and at Stoke Fleming near Dartmouth which had an ancient wayside cross. In the mid nineteenth century it had fallen into disrepair and was reused by a farmer, after he had broken off one arm, as a gate post. Afterwards it was acquired by the owner of nearby Sheplegh Court who resited it at Bow Bridge near his grounds as a curiosity. A subsequent owner of the building gave it to the parish to use for a memorial in May 1919 and it was restored and erected not long after.[187] The monument at Holne, an octagonal Gothic cross, incorporated the base of the ancient cross. It was taken from the church where it was being used as a font.[188] Clyst Hydon also had its ancient cross restored.[189]

Exeter's Herbert Read restored at least four ancient crosses including at Alphington near Exeter where the head of the cross had been found nearby and subsequently used for the new memorial.[190] Berry Pomeroy reused the base of its ancient cross with the additions again designed by Read but executed by a Totnes firm.[191] This was the same arrangement at Ipplepen where again Read provided the design and F. Horn

IN EVER LIVING MEMORY OF ALL
THOSE FROM THIS PARISH WHO
GAVE THEIR LIVES FOR GOD THEIR
COUNTRY AND US IN THE GREAT WAR

52. *The large monument at St Giles-in-the-Wood,*
*raised high in the viewer's gaze.*

53. *Brixham's cross with its runic design.*

54. *The war memorial cross at Ermington.*

55. *Another distinctive design is that created for the parishes of East and West Worlington.*

56. *The cross at Wembworthy also has an unusual design.*

undertook the work.[192] Likewise at Chagford the ancient cross was put to a new use. It had been removed and put to what was described as a utilitarian use: the base of the cross was used as a trough. The cross was restored by Read and placed in the new churchyard which was itself a gift from Thomas Amery in memory of his son who died in the war.[193]

The crosses took some forms which are clearly identifiable such as Latin, Celtic and Maltese crosses. The design was yet another of the choices which had to be made by local committees and they occasionally decided upon eccentric forms: the design for a war memorial cross at Broadhempston near Totnes was not described as a cross but as a monument which was to take the shape of a block of granite surmounted by a cross.[194] At Salcombe Regis in East Devon a vote was taken in a public meeting to decide the design of the cross. Fifteen members of the audience voted for a Cornish cross and nineteen for a Latin one. A further vote was held and seventeen wanted the figure of Jesus to be on the cross and twelve voted against.[195]

Latin crosses were one of the more common choices. In this design the arms are the same length as the top and it differed from a Calvary Cross in that it did not have three steps leading up to it. These are a feature of many of the crosses around Exeter in particular but can be found in parishes across Devon. They were not popular everywhere including in Ugborough where the war memorial committee rejected having a Latin cross and voted for what they called 'a Devon cross'.[196] Latin crosses could be seen as being too close to the Roman Catholic Church and some Devonians felt more comfortable with a design which they considered to be more local. Thus the cross at Ide was planned by the vicar who said at its unveiling that he designed it 'upon the lines of local Devonshire crosses such as stand at Alphington'.[197] Likewise, some of the war memorial crosses were intentionally erected as replicas of ancient crosses found elsewhere such as that at Walkhampton which was described at its unveiling as 'a copy of an old Devon cross'.[198] That at Whimple was based on the cross at Harpford[199] and Lifton's was a copy of a cross at Meavy.[200] That at Blundell's School in Tiverton is eighteen-feet high and carved of Correhill sandstone by Harry Hems & Sons of Exeter. It was a copy of the famous cross at Eyam in Derbyshire.[201] The parish of St Sidwell in Exeter had also discussed erecting a replica of that cross but was unable to finance it.[202]

Celtic crosses differ from Latin crosses only in that there is a ring surrounding the intersection. These were the choice of communities in every part of Devon. Some of them also have runes. One is that at Brixham which was described at its unveiling as being a 'runic cross'.[203] These may have been preferred in some communities because there was a popular understanding that Celtic crosses were distinctly British.[204] Maltese crosses are formed by the points of four arrow-heads meeting together and these were commonly erected. At Churston Ferrers near Brixham the committee originally wanted a Greek Cross but settled for a Maltese one.[205] Other war memorial crosses cannot be easily identified as being either Latin, Celtic, Runic or Maltese in their designs but specific to that village. Across Devon crosses were erected with creative designs.

These traditional forms of the cross were supplemented after the Great War by a new design. The Cross of Sacrifice was designed by Sir Reginald Blomfield, one of the principal architects with the Imperial War Graves Commission (later the Commonwealth War Graves Commission) for the design of cemeteries in Belgium and France. He was a Devonian, born at Bow near Crediton in 1856. Blomfield designed the Cross of Sacrifice which stands in the Commission's graves and would later design the Menin Gate at Ypres, the war memorial to the missing.[206] His cross was intended to 'speak of its own time'. The cross was severe with capped ends to each limb and a sword in bronze pointing downwards on its face. Blomfield regarded his design as one of simplicity and modernistic and unlike gothic or runic crosses which, he thought, had 'nothing to do with the grim terrors of the trenches'.[207] The strength of the design was due to the shared shape of the cross and the sword. There are at least ten swords which could be versions of his design in Devon but only one place in which Blomfield was involved.

Totnes attempted, and succeeded, in producing a monument far superior to other places of its size or of neighbouring communities. A committee first met in February 1919 and decided upon providing a recreation ground as a memorial. Various sites were investigated including an unsuccessful attempt to persuade the Duke of Somerset to lease Totnes Castle to the town and allow a stone memorial to be placed there. Within a few months it had become apparent that all schemes were hopeless and the committee agreed to only erect a stone monument. A subsequent meeting of the town council separately revived the notion of a recreation ground. Shortly afterwards it became apparent that even for a monument the committee had insufficient funds but it refused to openly canvas residents for money and instead voted to have the Mayor at the Guildhall to receive voluntary contributions and place boxes in public on market days. This brought in a meagre amount. The committee was then saved by two women from the Women's War Work and Moss Depot Committees coming forward. Through their efforts money poured into the fund. The committee was then able to pursue designs for a monument. They received four from throughout the country.[208] The Mayor also travelled to London to see the Cross of Sacrifice which had been erected at Burlington House and met Sir Reginald Blomfield. The committee agreed to a design by Blomfield and thus the town acquired the services of one of the leading artists in the memorial movement. He provided a plan, for a charge of ten per cent of the final cost of the cross, which was executed by Mr F. Horn, who at times called himself 'monumental and architectural stone mason', 'monumentalist' and 'monumental and architectural stone

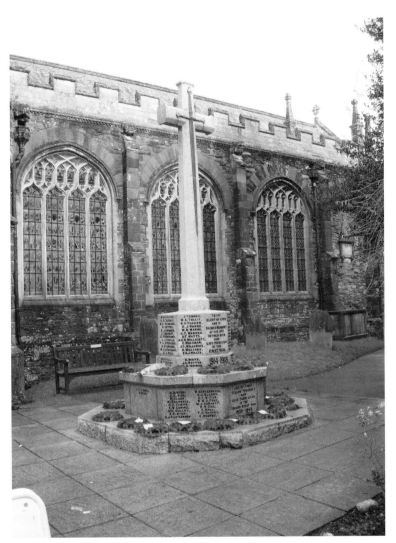

*57. Sir Reginald Blomfield's Sword of Sacrifice at Totnes.*

58. *The sword on Atherington's cross.*

*59. Colyton's sword on its cross.*

mason and sculptor', of Totnes. Blomfield preferred to use a Torquay mason in whose work he had confidence but agreed to work with Horn if the Committee could guarantee his competence.

60. *George Nympton also has an unusual sword motif.*

In the summer of 1920 a site was agreed: the cross was to
be placed on the right-hand side of the Anglican church facing
Fore Street. The Prince of Wales was invited to unveil the
monument but declined. Interestingly, the second option was

61. *The cross at Malborough near Salcombe is another design unique within Devon.*

not the Duke of Somerset but Lieutenant Colonel the Right Honourable F. B. Mildmay who was the town's Member of Parliament. The date set for the unveiling was June 4th 1921. On the morning of the unveiling the town's mayor, who had

62. *Some wall tablets have swords, such as this one at Braunton.*

played a leading role in organizing the monument, suddenly died. The ceremony still took place and the fifteen foot high stone cross was unveiled to a large crowd. Horn used Dartmoor granite despite Blomfield's concerns that the colour would be uneven. The latter had suggested using either Cornish granite or Portland stone.

At the unveiling the crowd was reminded the cross symbolised sacrifice and the sword was intended to symbolise service. Blomfield subsequently wrote 'that my design should really appeal to all who have suffered in this war was what I aimed at and hoped for from the first. The cross looks very well in its setting at Totnes'.[209]

Blomfield's design had became so popular that it became regarded as common property throughout the country.[210] The sword was a popular motif with a medieval lineage. In addition to Totnes, the crosses at Colyton, Iddesleigh, Lynton, Malborough, Milton Abbot and Witheridge have inscribed swords which faces downwards as Blomfield intended. In three, Atherington, George Nympton and Parkham, the swords point upwards. However, only on the Totnes cross is the sword made of bronze. These other possible versions of Blomfield's design were all carved from the same granite as the cross. Blomfield himself had said 'the design is, of course, my copyright but I have come across horrible travesties of it in many local memorials apparently executed by the local mason from illustrations of the cross given in the papers'.[211] He would have been more appalled had he known that most of the Devon crosses, on which were placed what might have been attempts to copy his Sword of Sacrifice, are Celtic Crosses.

Not all Devon places used the same term to describe the sword on their memorials. At Lynton it was used as Blomfield had intended. In 1923 the audience at the unveiling were reminded by one speaker that they stood under the 'great sword of sacrifice'.[212] However, in Devon it was generally not called a Sword of Sacrifice. At Colyton the sword was noted as 'of the pattern greatly used in France' and when it was unveiled a year later it was described by one newspaper as 'a crusader's cross in relief'.[213] The Milton Abbot cross was also said to have a crusader's cross when it was erected in 1921.[214] Iddesleigh erected a cross in 1920 with what was called a 'Crusader's

Cross' and also 'the Crusaders' Memorial'.[215] These places may have been resurrecting the analogy of the cross and medieval sword rather than as an imitation of Blomfield.[216] Malborough's cross has what was described as 'of Wallace cross design' when it was unveiled.[217] St Marychurch has a crossed sword and rifle.

Nearly all of the crosses were erected through public donations. A minority were raised by private individuals such as those already mentioned at Parkham and Ivybridge. In June 1919 Mr Trehawke Kekewich of Peamore near Exeter erected his own personal tribute to those that died in the Great War. A ten foot high cross, made of Devon granite, was situated along the public road outside his country house. It was inscribed only with the years of the conflict.[218] Less than seven months after the signing of the Truce the rector of Butterleigh erected a cross ten feet high in his churchyard. This was to honour the death of his youngest son.[219]

Many firms provided crosses within their own area such as Mr G. B. Andrews in his own town of Ivybridge, W. H. Fewings & Sons in its home town of Tiverton, Jenkins & Son of Torquay executed the cross at St Marychurch, W. C. Willis of Combe Martin executed that resort's monument and H. A. Gullet of Plympton did that for nearby Cornwood.[220] At Brixham the committee employed a firm of architects from nearby Paignton and the masons were from Brixham.[221] Two staff members of the Tiverton School of Art, Miss N. M. Nelder and Mr G. Pleace, were responsible for the carving of the great wooden tablet for Withleigh parish at Tiverton.[222] Other commissions came from a distance. The Crediton firm Dart & Francis executed Ashburton's memorial in the parish church.[223] The illustrious firm of Harry Hems & Son designed or executed many local crosses including those at Axmouth,[224] Awliscombe,[225] Chittlehampton,[226] East Budleigh,[227] East and West Worlington,[228] Parracombe[229] and Sidbury.[230] Another firm which was very active throughout Devon was Herbert Read's St Sidwell Artworks which erected crosses at such places as Axminster,[231] Peamore,[232] Buckerell,[233] Dean Prior,[234] Goodleigh,[235] Lapford,[236] and Walkhampton.[237] J. T. Miller of the Art Memorial Works in Okehampton provided memorial crosses at such places as Bow,[238] Chulmleigh,[239] Iddesleigh,[240] Lifton[241] Milton Abbot[242] and Petrockstowe[243] as well as Okehampton.[244] Many of the crosses were designed by one firm or individual and executed by another. This was the case with the cross at Milton Abbot: it was carved by Miller of Okehampton but was designed by T. C. Ratcliffe, the architect to the Duke of Bedford who owned considerable property in the parish.[245]

Some of the crosses were made of Cornish granite, such as at Awliscombe,[246] but the majority appears to have been carved of granite from Devon. Notable exceptions include that at Lynton, which is of Peterhead red granite, the cross at Blundell's School was carved from pink marble, the cross at Upottery came from the Doulton quarry in Somerset, that of St John's church in Plymouth is of Bath stone[247] and that at Cove was carved of red granite from an unknown quarry.[248] There seems to have been a preference to use local stone, and workmen, when possible. At Newton Abbot the sculptor was told 'we must adhere, if we can, to the principle Devon stone for a Devon Memorial but this point need not be considered rigid'.[249] Near Dartmouth, in the parish of Stoke Fleming, the committee did not just want Devon craftsmen but ones local to them.[250]

## The Devon County cross and Sir Edwin Lutyens

Devon's most prestigious cross was erected by Devon County Council in 1921. It engaged Sir Edwin Lutyens, the foremost designer at that time who had created the national monument, the Cenotaph, which had instigated the war memorial movement. The erection of the cross came after two years of rivalry between the councils of the county of Devon and the city of Exeter.

63. *Sir Edwin Lutyens' monument
within Cathedral Yard at Exeter.*

In December 1919 the county council unveiled its plans for a cross near Exeter Cathedral. This was a prime position within the cathedral precincts and would be the most prominent site for any of Exeter's memorials. For Exeter it was the equivalent of the navy monument on the Hoe in Plymouth. Even so, it was reported by one newspaper that there were concerns that the West Quarter's residents, categorised as thoughtless and irresponsible people, might abuse the area if it was opened to public use.[251] The reference to these residents, who lived in the poorest part of the city which was only a few hundred yards away, was repeated in a report to the cathedral authorities two years later which warned of the 'undesirable characters' who met at night outside St Petrock's Church.[252]

The choice of a cross had not been easy. A month after the cessation of hostilities, in December 1918, the Dean of Exeter took the initiative by suggesting that rebuilding the Cloisters was the most appropriate way to mark those who had died in the war. Dean Gamble wrote to 'leading persons connected with the diocese' asking for their financial support[253] but the necessary funds were not found and the scheme was abandoned two months later. He later suggested the public was unwilling partly because money was already pledged to more local memorials which he felt were often of a 'somewhat trivial character'.[254] It had been suggested that within the cloisters could stand a monument thought up by Earl Fortescue, Lord Lieutenant of Devon. He envisaged a granite pedestal on which would be placed the muzzles of captured German guns. The early weeks of 1919 had seen media speculation with the two leading contenders being the rebuilt Cloisters or erecting a wing at the Royal Devon & Exeter Hospital.[255] Neither would form the official county monument.

In early July 1919 a county-appointed committee, headed by Fortescue, considered the options. A letter from the earl had appeared in local newspapers in which he asked for suggestions. Twenty-three ideas were offered and the committee's discussions revealed deep divisions similar to those simmering across Devon. The majority of the committee were establishment figures; many came from the great landed families or were magistrates or politicians. The Church of England was represented by the Dean and Prebendary Buckingham. This group argued for an ornamental memorial. A minority, which included a representative of the independent churches and another for the soldiers, wanted a functional memorial. The larger group disparagingly called this a 'public utility' memorial and voted against it. The subsequent members of the executive committee, who were decided upon at the meeting, were drawn solely from the majority group.[256]

The twenty-three public suggestions included annuities to widows and orphans, a soldiers' club, schemes to provide for servicemen and their dependents, a Nurses Naval Hospital, a Children's Home for Servicemen, a cottage for wounded pensioners, and houses for Disabled Soldiers and Sailors. The Executive Committee only considered inscribing marble monuments for each Anglican church porch, completing Exeter Cathedral's cloisters, or erecting monuments, in the form of crosses, crucifixes or obelisks, in either Exeter, Dartmoor, Haldon or Cawsand Beacon.[257]

Within weeks debate had largely ceased although the general committee met at Rougemont Castle, where Devon County Council was based, and Mr Walters, of the Federation of Discharged and Demobilised Soldiers and Sailors, again advocated a 'living memorial': he asked the committee for 'the establishment and maintenance of an institute for clothing, feeding and educating the children of men who had fallen in the war'. Nevertheless, Fortescue announced shortly afterwards it had decided upon a cross in Cathedral Close, a book of honour, and a financial contribution to the monument being erected in France to the Devonshire Regiment.[258] The design was announced as 'the simple form of a Cenotaph surmounted by a cross similar to those being erected in France'.[259] Even before this meeting the Dean & Chapter had discussed the

Architect's Office,
Raisina,
DELHI.

Jan. 18. 22.

Dear Mr. Ford,

Very many thanks for your letter of Dec. 16 with the plan and enclosure from Mr. Harbottle.

I am very glad your Committee realise how badly the Green requires treatment to give due dignity to the War Memorial.

I do not think any solution will be satisfactory if the iron railings are left.    Would it not be possible to get tenders to remove the railings and to give credit for them, lay a granite path, turf, and plant trees.

I do not think shrubs or any form of gardening would be suitable.

I think, too, that gate posts with an inscription so near would inflict conflict and detract from the simplicity of the Cross.

St. Mary Major's Church is in a terrible position and makes the problem very difficult.

Mr. Thomas at 17 Queen Annes Gate will help you to get tenders, and if necessary without advertisement. The iron railings must be of value to someone in need of such material.

Could not the wall round St. Mary Major's Church be removed as well ?

Yours very truly,

Edwin L. Lutyens.

*64. Letter from Sir Edwin Lutyens at Dehli regarding his Exeter monument, 1922.*

possibility of a cross and decided it had no objection if the county wanted to erect one.[260] By November the site near the cathedral was offered.[261]

By summer 1919 the rivalry between the county and city councils over war memorials was made public. Early that year hopes were expressed for a joint memorial but by July each council had decided upon being independent. A county council representative was at pains to express that discussions and relations were 'entirely friendly' and that 'there was no slamming of doors or anything of that sort' but it is clear there was antagonism.[262] Exeter City Council announced its memorial plans shortly before Devon County Council made its plans known. In its announcement the City Council publicly 'cordially invited the cooperation' of the County Council in raising funds for what they stressed would be the 'one central monument in the capital and centre of Devon'.[263] That month it became clear that both councils wanted to take the lead and have the other merely contribute funds. It was also apparent that neither would allow the other to take precedence. There would be no collaboration.

The executive committee made the decisions regarding the monument and the Cathedral authorities restricted themselves to commenting on its erection. In the summer of 1919 the council hired Lutyens who was then in India. In May 1920 Lutyens came to Exeter on his return from Dehli and discussed the exact position of the cross.[264] He chose Dartmoor granite from Haytor and the quarry reopened to provide stone for the cross.

On Whitsun Monday, 17 May 1921, Edward Prince of Wales was greeted by thousands of local people as he travelled through the streets of Exeter to unveil the memorial. He first stopped at the Guildhall where he told the assembled councillors who were dressed in their scarlet robes:

'Today we have a sad and proud duty to perform – sad because the unveiling of a war memorial awakens most sorrowful memories in all our hearts, proud because every heart must thrill in recalling the glorious record of the sons of Devon in the great war . . .'

The Prince then walked through Broadgate to Lutyen's cross and told the waiting crowd:

'I know what this memorial means here in Exeter and Devon, and I feel sure that it will serve as a great inspiration to coming generations to do their best in whatever way they may be called upon and so uphold those splendid traditions which have been handed down by generations of the men of Devon'.

The inscription that he read was 'The county of Devon to her glorious dead, 1914–1919' followed by, in Latin, 'You God, we praise'. As the prince passed through Exeter he saw printed greetings including one that read 'You'm welcome, Prince. Us be praper glad to zee-e'.[265] A memorial book was prepared of the 11,796 names of the men and women of Devon who had died in the war. The Prince unveiled it.

The 'Simple Cross' was a design Lutyens used in one other city, York, as well as at Stockbridge in Hampshire and Abinger Common in Surrey.[266] His design was criticised in the *Express & Echo* by one journalist who thought it looked like a 'slender finger pointing upwards' with beautiful lines but not characteristic of Devon. He had examined the cross before the unveiling and reported that other Exonians gathered around it were as disappointed as he. In his opinion it was too airy and unsubstantial although he conceded it was Whitehall's Cenotaph in miniature. The cross, he wrote, resembled a sword blade.[267] The design is overwhelmed itself by the site and the cathedral. The county council was undoubtedly proud of having engaged the leading war memorial artist of the time but the result was modest and unassuming compared to those of the Royal Navy at Plymouth or that which would be erected by its near rival, the City of Exeter. That monument was a stark contrast to Lutyen's cross and would become Exeter's foremost war memorial.

## Secular monuments in the landscape

Some communities decided against a cross, in many cases because they did not want a religious symbol but still wanted a freestanding monument. A few made unusual choices, such as Pyworthy, which has a sundial. The town of Crediton produced one of the most curious monuments in Devon. It was a little tardy in erecting a memorial than surrounding villages but in keeping with other towns, not until 1923, but the result was eye-catching. At the time it was described as 'an octagonal column around which is built a pent house, the whole being surmounted by a slender spire with a cross at the apex. The shelter, as it might be termed, is supported by eight oak pillars on stone pediments and around the central support is a stone seat.' It was also described as reminiscent of an old market building. The monument was designed by Frederick Bligh Bond, a descendant of Captain Bligh of HMS *Bounty*. Although an established architect Bligh was a controversial choice. He became known for his interest in spiritualism and claimed to have used mediums in his archaeological work at Glastonbury Abbey. Bligh was dismissed by the diocese of Bath & Wells and shortly afterwards was employed at Crediton. The cost of his Crediton monument, which included a tablet in the church, was £1,800 which exceeded other comparable Devon towns.[268] Most of the other secular freestanding memorials in Devon took the form of obelisks, columns or cenotaphs.

There is no single part of Devon where obelisks are more prevalent; they were erected throughout the county, in both urban and rural areas and in all geographical parts of Devon, including at Chudleigh, Culmstock, Doddiscombesleigh, Germansweek, Halwill, Harbertonford, Higher Tale, Kenton, Loddiswell, Mary Tavy, Modbury, Monkleigh, Northam,

65. *Crediton's unusual war memorial whose designer
was later consecrated a bishop in the Old Catholic Church
in the United States.*

66. *The obelisk at Culmstock, an ambitious monument for the village.*

North Tawton, Paignton, Plympton St Maurice, Rackenford, Sheepwash, Swimbridge and Teignmouth. The latter obelisk was derided by one resident as:

'at best a Pagan object whilst a cross of some kind, such as thousands of other places are having, is a Christian emblem, and suggests the sacrifice that the memorials are intended to perpetuate. The lads who died gave their lives for Christian ideals. Why should any town shy at the idea of erecting a cross, which is both pretty attractive, to their glorious memory?'[269]

Another resident wrote it was an offence to the eyesight and that nothing could be uglier.[270]

One man thought:

'The boys who died gave their lives for Christian ideals. Why cannot we perpetuate their memory by a Christian symbol rather than a Pagan one? The obelisk belongs to an Egyptian heathenism; the cross is an emblem of Christian hope.'[271]

In contrast, it does not seem to have been thought offensive in Monkleigh where an obelisk was erected as a war memorial in the churchyard. Nor could it have offended the rector of Plympton St Maurice given he designed one as the parish memorial. What is particularly interestingly about his obelisk was that it was also described as a pylon by which was meant the gateway of an ancient Egyptian temple. His design includes crosses at the two sides where the sun rises and sets. The designer of Torquay's monument also described it as a pylon.[272]

Across Devon there had been many obelisks erected as personal grave monuments without any apparent association as pagan objects before the Great War and they were an established form for victory memorials throughout the country.[273] One was proposed as a war memorial at Ilfracombe

67. *Germansweek's obelisk sits within its own recreational ground.*

in 1919 on one of the most prominent places in the resort: one resident suggested Capstone Hill and offered £250 towards it. Another resident responded by saying it would look like a Cornish mining chimney.[274] The disparaging of obelisks at Teignmouth and Ilfracombe was opposite to the opinion

68. *North Tawton's memorial was placed within a small park which has become a cemetery.*

expressed in Paignton by an official who said an obelisk could offend no one. He suggested there was no other form more suitable for a war monument than an obelisk.[275] The *Western Times* does not seem to have regarded obelisks as having any religious overtones: it merely regarded the one unveiled in

69. *Paignton's obelisk of which it was hoped could offend no one.*

1920 at Appledore in North Devon as 'a beautiful piece of work'.[276]

The size of obelisks varied as those did of crosses. Some were tall structures such as that at Swimbridge near Barnstaple which stands at twelve feet[277] and others were much smaller

70. *Teignmouth's obelisk which was highly
controversial when it was erected.*

such as the one which stands at Tale in East Devon. The designs also varied as considerably as those for crosses. The parishioners of Willand near Cullompton chose an obelisk which was surmounted by a lamp.[278] The memorial at Thorverton's was described when it was unveiled as a column and yet it has a cross, albeit a small one, at its apex.[279] They could also be the work of several individuals: that at North Tawton was designed by a local man, Samuel Sampson of nearby Wildridge, and executed by Mr Osborne of nearby South Zeal.[280]

The grandest of all the Devon obelisks or columns is that which was erected on the Hoe in Plymouth for the Royal Navy. The Hoe was the most conspicuous place to erect a monument and it was sited here for maximum public impact. It was the point where the public gathered for public occasions and where existing monuments to the Armada and the South African wars were already situated. The memorial takes the

71. *A cenotaph was suggested as Plymouth's City Memorial. The proposer thought the word Remembrance should be inscribed on the southern side and the date of the war on the north. The effect would be to have to have the date symbolically in shadow and Remembrance lit by the sun throughout the year.*

72. *Another proposed design for Plymouth.*

shape of a massive stone obelisk supported by four corner buttresses and stands at more than one hundred feet high. The monument was erected by the Imperial War Graves Commission to honour naval men who were lost from the port and it was unveiled in 1924. It was then the second of three identical memorials to be erected: one had already been built at Chatham and the third was under construction at Portsmouth. Their design was altered in each place following the Second World War. The monument was regarded as both a seamark and a landmark. Some 25,000 people attended the unveiling in that summer.[281]

This structure has at the top bronze figures representing the Four Winds of Heaven. Above these is a copper sphere meant to depict the globe and around the base are four sculptured lions. Prince George unveiled the monument on July 29th and said that each name engraved in bronze represents part of the price paid by the Empire.[282] It honours the memory of the naval men of Plymouth and still stands as the tallest memorial ever erected in Devon with one exception: one hundred years earlier the Devonport column was erected and this stands at 124 feet. The effect is one of inspiration and while it may have comforted the bereaved it also honoured the navy as a whole: the memorial towers over the viewer and makes the viewer aware that each of the dead was part of a vast service. In

73. *Plymouth had a number of suggested designs.*

74. *Plymouth's greatest memorial was erected on the Hoe in 1924 to honour those who died in the Royal Navy.*

*75. One of the magnificent stone lions.*

exalting the dead and glorifying in their service the size of the monument also emphasised the nobility or justice of the war's cause. It is a muscular monument designed by men to honour men but intended to address mourners who were principally women. The monument forms part of a collection of other war memorials but it effectively dwarfs all the rest.

There are also pillars or columns in such places as Huish, Lynton, Newton Abbot, Noss Mayo, Rousdon and Torquay. Dodbrooke has an ingenious memorial which has been placed near the entrance to the church graveyard. The inscription on it reads 'the above pillar for centuries stood in the church. The top base formed part of the ancient wayside cross'. The monument at Sheepwash is even less elaborate: it comprises a plain granite shaft eleven feet high.[283] Halwill's obelisk is by comparison much more accomplished with its decorative cap. That at Noss Mayo is the only one that mimics a common

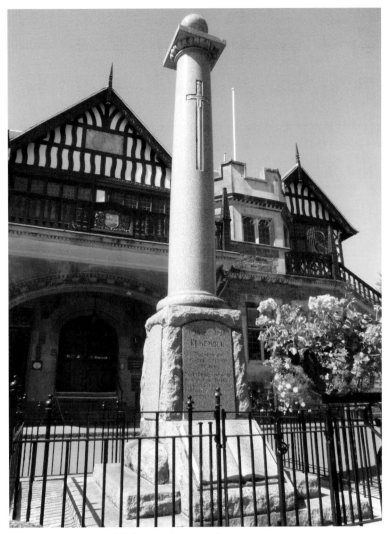

*76. Lynton's unusual monument.*

Victorian graveyard motif: it has a broken column, to signify death before its time.

One of the greatest of the county's memorials was erected in Devonport in 1923 and comprises a thirty-three feet

123

77. *The re-used church stone which was fashioned
into a Great War monument at Dodbrooke.*

78. *The Devonport monument, a testament to the civic pride of a town once larger than the city of Exeter.*

79. *The Great War monument at Axminster with
St George slaying the dragon.*

high pedestal of Cornish granite which is capped with an
ornamental lantern surmounted by a cross. The figure of
Victory stands at the base of the shaft. The monument was
designed by Charles Cheverton of London and commemorates
the more than 2,000 Devonport men and women who died

126

80. *The cenotaph at Moretonhampstead has*
*unusual decoration around its cross.*

81. *Sir Edwin Blomfield's magnificent pylon at Torquay.*

in the Great War. It is interesting that Devonport erected a column given that 99 years before it already had built its great column, one of the great symbols of the town. Devonport, as one of the three towns, had just merged with Plymouth to form the borough of Plymouth in 1914. Even so, there was residual local pride. One newspaper noted that the inhabitants were jealously keeping their separate identity and had refused to join with Plymouth in erecting a monument. They even refused the offer of unveiling their monuments on the same day. On one side was placed the old Devonport borough's coat of arms. Nevertheless, the mayor of Plymouth attended the unveiling. Devonport's memorial was one of the most expensive in Devon: it cost some £1,500. The unveiling had a feature which was unusual for its time: the air force flew two airplanes from Lee-on-Solent as its tribute.[284]

There are at least three cenotaphs in Devon and several others which have not survived although it needs to be understood that the word described a concept and not a design. The Cenotaph in London bore little resemblance to those later called by that name in Devon. Whereas that in London was meant to imply a sarcophagus or a coffin lying in state,[285] the word became used to describe in general a simple monument symbolic of mourning. Both Sidmouth and Exmouth erected what they called cenotaphs as temporary memorials in 1920.[286] In 1919 the planned County memorial at Exeter was described as a cenotaph surmounted by a cross but it has nothing in common with the national Cenotaph other than having been designed by the same man.[287] Moretonhampstead has a monument which was also described at the unveiling as a cenotaph.[288]

In 1921 the borough of Torquay unveiled its grand war monument along the seafront. It stands as the most impressive cenotaph in Devon. The design was by Sir Reginald Blomfield who was also working at the same time on the memorial cross for Totnes. Blomfield's monument stands at approximately thirty feet high and was composed of Portland stone. Unusually for Devon it lists the war dead under the three services of

82. *Luton's monument which is the same design as at Torquay.
The difference lies with the figure of Victory.*

the army, navy and air force. It also features bronze wreaths and inverted torches. The monument cost more than £2,000, one of the most expensive memorials in Devon. It was widely described as a cenotaph at the time but Blomfield himself later wrote:

130

'I designed, among others, three important memorials on the "pylon" motif, that is, a lofty pedestal with a symbol of the purpose of the memorial, the first was at Torquay.'

The borough had attempted to have a figure of Victory, like that which was on Luton's version of Torquay's memorial but could not raise the extra funds.[289] Plympton St Maurice erected Devon's last Great War cenotaph, or pylon as mentioned earlier, in May 1924.[290]

## Figurative Monuments

There are relatively few figurative Great War monuments in Devon and of them Kingsbridge has Hope while Northam has Liberty but Devonport, Exeter, Ilfracombe, Newton Abbot and Plymouth each have Victory. Each of these places erected figurative monuments in contrast to all the other urban areas of Devon. There was some discussion of figures for other places but the plans were not realised. Torquay, for instance, wanted a statue of Victory surmounting its cenotaph but it ended up with a flame. One Paigntonian wanted a statue of 'the Empire Mother'. She would be seated, draped 'in flowing folds, holding on the knees a scroll bearing the word *Promoted*. The square column beneath it inscribed with the names and placed within a semi-circle of evergreen'.[291] Brixham's preferred monument in 1919 had been a clock-tower surmounted by a statue of Liberty. It had also considered a column with a bronze figure of Victory but eventually erected a cross.[292] Victory is the most common figure to be found in Britain's Great War monuments[293] and Devon conforms to the tradition of her carrying a wreath and sword.

There are few other figures besides Victory, Hope and Liberty. Many of the figurative stone monuments could be described as masculine in their general design but the artists chose not to have a male figure, such as St George, and instead opted for a feminine one. This may have been done to avoid religious associations but also to have a contrast with the men

83. *Liberty at Northam, an unusual figure for Devon.*

that the stones were commemorating. Male figures were used exclusively for the Devonshire Regiment memorial and only partly for the City of Exeter. Even the figures of the wind for the Royal Naval monument are female.

The one Devon place which achieved a figure of Liberty was

84. *Hope is another figure which was a curious choice for Kingsbridge to have made for its town monument.*

Northam near Bideford. It erected one of the county's most unusual monuments: it has Liberty standing on a stone pillar. The figure may have been intended to refer to two of Britain's allies during the war; Liberty has associations with France

*85. Newton Abbot's monument.*

and its Marianne as well as New York's Statue of Liberty which was a gift of the French government.[294] The figurative memorials at Ilfracombe, Kingsbridge, Newton Abbot and Northam use their columns as pedestals in the same manner as classical hero statues. Broken chains are also a feature of the figures with them appearing at Exeter, Kingsbridge and Newton Abbot. The sculptured figures are all either British or

86. *Victory modelled by a French woman.*

allegorical whereas the stained glass, because it was erected in religious buildings, depict either British or biblical figures particularly military saints. There are no depictions of the conquered in Devon.

Kingsbridge is unique in Devon in having a war memorial with a statue of Hope. It was unveiled in November 1925, the last of Devon's towns to erect a monument. The stone monument appeared six years after the town's aforementioned first memorial, a recreation ground. By 1925 it is likely the statue Hope was chosen instead of Victory in order not to appear triumphant. By that date there was dissatisfaction with the lengthy delay and a local newspaper commented that Kingsbridge was one of the few towns not to have a public monument and it would have been a disgrace had it not.[295]

In the autumn of 1920 Newton Abbot decided to erect what was described as a version of Nelson's Column with a figure of Victory surmounting it. It had taken the town more than a year to agree on which type of memorial it wanted and several more years would pass before the monument was erected. They chose Courtenay Pollock to create the figure of Victory. Pollock introduced himself as a local man with an international profile.

'Though my work has been done mainly in my studio in London and New York, my home is Devon and I should therefore feel it an honour to have the opportunity of making a bronze figure for your memorial if you have not already selected a sculptor. I have spent a great deal of my life in Torquay where I have a house, and my grandfather before me lived there also, so I think my claim to be a Devon sculptor will be allowed.'[296]

Pollock actually lived in Ilfracombe and the committee became impatient at what they saw as long delays in finishing the monument. He responded that artists and craftsmen were unable to meet the demand of the war memorial commissions and that he had five months of illness in which he 'narrowly escaped crossing the Styx'. He even wrote a public apology for the delay which he sent to local newspapers. Pollock also had trouble finding a suitable model to pose for his nude sculpture.

'I may say that I have had the greatest difficulty in getting a good model, though I tried Exeter, Ilfracombe, Torquay,

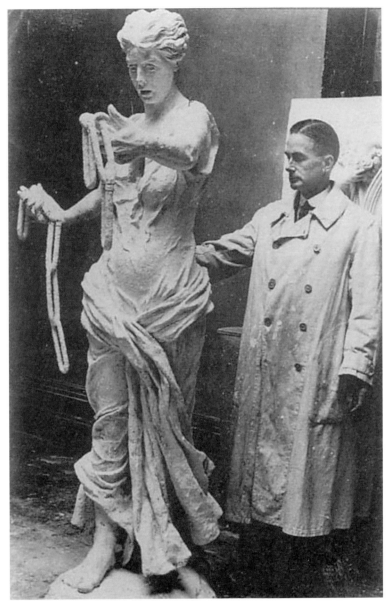

87. *Mr Pollock with his Victory.*

88. *Ilfracombe's monument,*
*also designed by Courtenay Pollock.*

89. *Ilfracombe's Victory, most probably modelled by the same French woman who posed for Newton Abbot's memorial.*

Bristol and London. Excepting in London there was no model to be had. Finally I was offered the only female figure model in London who was free. I had her down, paid her expenses and fees, and sent her back again as her figure was useless to me. I at last found a suitable one. But so difficult is to get the proper model, I have had to engage her permanently in order to secure one.'[297]

The model he found was French.[298] At one point the committee refused to send any further money until the figure was finished and they also sent a series of questions for him to answer. Most of them he answered in good nature with one strong exception. The committee advised him to obtain a number of estimates for work. They were told 'Mr Pollock believes he is capable of conducting his profession without amateur advice.' The monument was eventually unveiled to great acclaim with

90. *Plymouth City's monument with its main mannish figure, Victory.*

the figure pointed out for particular praise. Interestingly, at one point Pollock referred to his figure not as Victory but as Freedom.[299]

Pollock's technique was to create a nude statue and then drape it with clothing. Interestingly, his Newton Abbot

140

91. *Victory who stands, in tears, at the base of the Devonport monument.*

statue was clothed unlike his other Devon figure which was located in distant part of the county. The North Devon resort of Ilfracombe also employed Pollock. It took the form of a granite column surmounted by another bronze winged figure of Victory.[300] His design was markedly similar to the

141

92. *The Royal Marines' monument at Plymouth Hoe.*

93. *One of the two carved stone figures.*

94. *One marine looks out to sea.*

95. *The main figure is a young man who is struggling with the eagle of militarism. The eagle's wing has wrapped around the nude youth giving him the appearance of an angel.*

143

TO THE GLORY OF GOD AND IN PROUD MEMORY OF THE GALLANT LADS
FROM THIS PARISH WHO GAVE THEIR LIVES IN THE GREAT WAR.
THOMAS H.BOND. P.O. I.Cl. H.M.S. OCEAN. SEPT. 14. 1914. AGED 42.
ALBERT W.CORNISH. C.Q.M.S. I.Devons. SEPT. 19. 1914. AGED 36.
GEORGE COWELL. SGT R.E. M.M. SEPT. 30. 1918. AGED 30.
FRANK H.R.EVANS. LCE CPL P.P.C.L.I. APRIL 14. 1916. AGED 23.
HARRY HAWKINS. GR R.G.A. M.M. DEC. 5. 1917. AGED 31.
FREDERICK E.HAWKINS. PTE 2.DEVONS. MAR. 10. 1915. AGED 26.
JOHN O.HAYMAN. SGT A.S.C. APRIL 21. 1916. AGED 23.
SIDNEY H.LOMAX. CPL R.E. AUG. 22. 1917. AGED 26.
JESSE H.MARSH. SGT 6. SOM. L.I. SEPT. 16. 1916. AGED 27.
JOHN MARTIN. 2. LIEUT. R.G.A. DEC. 19. 1917. AGED 25.
FRANK NORTON. PTE NORD FUS. APRIL 28. 1917. AGED 36.
ALFRED ROWE. R.N.V.R. OCT. 22. 1918. AGED 18.
HERBERT J.ROWE. PTE 8.DEVONS. JULY 20. 1916. AGED 19.
SYDNEY W.SMITH. PTE WORCS JAN. 14. 1917. AGED 39.
ERNEST J.STONEMAN. PTE M.G.C. MAY 29. 1917. AGED 20.
CHARLES J.SYMONS. BUGLER 5.DEVONS. OCT. 18. 1915. AGED 17.
WILLIAM J.TUBB. PTE 1.DEVONS. OCT. 28. 1914. AGED 32.
GEORGE W.H.TUCKER. DR R.F.A. AUG. 30. 1918. AGED 22.
DUTY NOBLY DONE.

1939 – 1945.
TO THE GLORY OF GOD & IN PROUD & CHERISHED MEMORY OF
ERNEST GEORGE BORDER.
AGED 18 YEARS. PTE 2ND DEVONS. WHO GAVE HIS LIFE IN THE
SERVICE OF HIS KING & COUNTRY IN THE SECOND WORLD WAR.

Offerings
for the work of the church

*96. The tablet in Abbotskerswell Anglican church was the work
of W. H. Crossman, stone and marble mason of Newton Abbot.
It features two figures, one of a sailor with HMS Devonshire
and the other a soldier of the Devonshire Regiment.*

one he had created at Newton Abbot. Interestingly, just as
he was finishing that for Newton Abbot he was also working
on the Ilfracombe figure. Pollock wrote to the committee in
the former town complaining that someone with a grudge
from Newton Abbot was disparaging his work amongst the
committee at Ilfracombe.[301]

97. *The Devonshire Regiment soldier at Abbotskerswell.*

98. *The* HMS Devonshire *sailor at Abbotskerswell*

Perhaps of all the figurative monuments in Devon, Plymouth City's is the least accomplished. It was situated at the Hoe on the junction of Lockyer Street and Citadel Road and unveiled in May 1923. It took the form of a low wall with a central pedestal on top of which is a figure of Victory. She holds a laurel wreath in one hand and a sword pointing downwards on the other. Her face was crudely executed by Birnie Rhind, a Scottish sculptor whose other work, including such memorials as that the King's Own Scottish Borderer's in Edinburgh, demonstrated his abilities more clearly. Lord Derby unveiled Plymouth's monument. He was there in his capacity of Secretary of State for War but one local newspaper stated he would be better styled Minister for Peace. At the unveiling Derby stated 'the great significance of the war memorial is only partly in tribute to the noble men who died. It is also a reminder to future generations that war can be waged only at a great price and heavy toll of the best blood of the nation.' He concluded that in that respect war memorials were a deterrent to future war. Some five hundred bouquets and wreaths were then laid on the memorial.[302] The memorial benefits from being placed at some distance from Plymouth other war memorials, notably that by erected by the navy.

In terms of being an accomplished piece of work, yet another nearby monument overshadows that of the City of Plymouth. In November 1921 the memorial to Plymouth's Royal Marines was unveiled on the Hoe. It is a surprising work of three figures. The idea for the monument originated with W. G. Storr-Barber, a former sculptor who was then enlisted in the marine corps. He offered to produce a war monument and continued the work when he was demobbed. He carved two striking figures of Portland stone and cast one in bronze. On either side of the main figure are two marines who express their motto, *Per Mare, Per Terram*, that is, By sea, by land. The sea figure is a marine dressed in a shirt and trousers whilst holding a gunner's ramrod and with bare arms. The second, a rifleman, wears a great coat and helmet. The main figure in the centre, which stands on a square pedestal, was variously described as an athlete or St George fighting the eagle of militarism. The sculptor said at the time that he thought the figures would last a hundred years but the two supporting marines were replaced in 1980 because of erosion.[303]

## The City of Exeter & John Angel

Exeter's official memorial is the most remarkable figurative monument in the county. It was unveiled in 1923 after four years of planning. Early in 1919 the mayor had dined with prominent citizens to solicit opinions on what might be achieved. The national Office of Works had instructed councils not to put up 'atrocities' and because of that the city was visited by Sir Reginald Blomfield.[304]

Blomfield was not given a commission but at one point the council called him the 'designer in chief'. By mid March the city had agreed to a 'statuary group' as a memorial. They were, no doubt, trying to sufficiently distinguish it from Lutyen's cross being undertaken by Devon County Council. A month after Blomfield's visit the mayor received a letter from John Angel, a local sculptor who was establishing himself in London. Angel asked if he could submit a design. Four months later, in July 1919, the War Memorial Committee accepted his proposal with the understanding that they had yet to raise the estimated five thousand pounds. They announced Angel was the sculptor along with the intended inscription 'To the proud memory of all men and women of Exeter and of Devon who gave their lives for England during the Great War, 1914 – 1918'.[305] This inscription, and the announcement itself, was a highly-charged political decision and the monument itself became, not surprisingly, controversial.

Even the choice of Angel became contentious. The Exeter monument was his first major work. He was one of twelve children, had lived in St Thomas and after leaving school at thirteen he worked in a coal merchant's office where his employer noted he was prone to drawing on his blotting paper

99. *John Angel's extraordinary monument
for the City of Exeter.*

and on odd scraps of paper. Angel then trained as an artist at the Art School while being apprenticed as a carver in wood and stone with J. Wippel & Company. For a short time Angel also worked in Herbert Read's workshop.[306] Angel's preliminary drawing of the monument was exhibited in the High Street and the *Express & Echo* suggested that it was not 'of a boastful, vain glorious, triumph but rather of thankfulness for dangers escaped, by the aid of Divine Providence.' A rival paper, the *Devon & Exeter Daily Gazette*, was not as supportive.[307] The nature of the coverage may have been due to the *Express & Echo's* editor being Sir James Owen, the city's wartime mayor.[308] Angel was immediately and repeatedly criticised by readers of the rival *Gazette*. One deplored the lack of a competition to decide an artist. Others were derisory of the semi-nudity of Angel's figures, one thought it was scandalous an airman was not one of the four figures, another wanted a 'less gaudy' design and yet one more suggested the city should merely have a replica of the Cenotaph. Another reader thought it was an unfortunate copy of a famous German monument.[309]

The Committee responded to the criticism by conceding the design could be modified and by the spring of 1920 Angel had made a sketch model which showed some changes. A visitor to his London studio reported:

'The figure representing womanhood – a Nurse – has gained in breadth and dignity. The soldier is in uniform now, treated on massive lines. The Sailor figure typifies the watch and ward which our fighting men, and men of the mercantile marine, kept on the seas for four long, weary years. And the Prisoner of War figure speaks endurance in every line.'[310]

There was later criticism that Angel took too long to create the memorial but the committee reportedly refused to hurry him.[311]

Two figures featured at the Royal Academy Show in May

100. *At the top, on a pedestal of Dartmoor granite, stands*
*Victory on top of a slain dragon. She is eight feet high*
*and the entire sculpture stands at 31 feet.*

101. *The soldier, facing Queen Street, wears a shrapnel helmet, overcoat and gas mask with a rifle slung over his shoulder.*

102. *The sailor looks towards the City Wall and sits astride the hull of a ship with the figurehead the city's coat of arms. He holds a submarine net in one hand and in the other a chart.*

103. *The third figure, facing north towards the prison, is the Prisoner of War.*

104. *The fourth figure is the V.A.D. Nurse and she holds*
*a bandage while at her side is a sheaf of corn and a shrapnel shell.*

1922. That of Victory, sometimes also known as Peace and also as Courage, stood in the courtyard of Burlington House[312] while the Prisoner of War was in the Sculpture Hall. These two were cast by the firm Thames Ditton located outside London while the remaining three figures were from the foundry of William Morris of Brixton.[313] Victory was the first figure to be cast[314] and of her one reviewer wrote it was the best exhibit in the Academy Show ('should not be missed') and of Angel his was 'a name unfamiliar to the art world and to the public at large. It is not likely to remain so.'[315]

There was also an ongoing debate in Exeter as to where the monument should be placed. A public meeting considered options and decided to try to acquire a site in Bedford Circus which meant that either the monument was simplified or the removal of the existing statue of the Earl of Devon. The city councillors overrode the initial decision and chose Northernhay Park. Their decision provoked a public call for all the subscribers to be polled and one prominent citizen asked for his donation to be returned.[316] There was further debate as to the best position in the park and the council adopted the site recommended by Angel in 1920.[317]

The memorial was paid for through a public appeal and more than £5,000 was raised in the first year.[318] One of the mottoes used was 'Every Little Helps'. A grant of £1,500 was given by the Lady Mayoress from her Prisoner of War Fund on condition that one figure was that of a prisoner of war.[319] There had been uncertainty as to whether this figure might be a land worker.[320] Altogether there were more than 15,000 subscribers, many of whom were children. The final cost was £6,350.[321]

In August 1922 William Morris wrote from his foundry to thank Angel for the contract to cast 'A Soldier' in bronze. His fee was three hundred pounds. Ten months later it, along with the Nurse, was ready for despatching to Exeter.[322] The site prepared early in 1923 and ready early that summer.[323] Finally, on the 24th of July, Lord Beatty, Admiral of the Fleet, arrived to unveil the memorial. He was also made an Honorary Freeman.[324]

Admiral Beatty said at the unveiling in July:

'. . . a time will come when the war will be but a faint echo down the path of time, and it is against that day that I feel we erect enduring memorials in stone and bronze to replace those who are enshrined in our hearts. Those who pass this memorial a generation hence, and generations after that, will not be stirred with the sense of personal pride and sadness which we feel, but they will see in it a reminder of the virtues which preserved this land, this Empire of ours', from disruptions in time of great peril. It will serve as a reminder of the courage and the self-sacrifice of their fathers, and as an incentive to spur them to equal nobility of purpose and action. History books will tell the story, and those who follow on will read with the same pride of England's part in the Great War as we read the exploits of bygone days. But a memorial such as this, erected to the citizens of their own City, will ensure that the England of the future recognises the debt which it owes to them . . .'[325]

Shortly afterwards the council passed a resolution that they 'congratulate Mr Angel on the completion of the War Memorial and do express their appreciation on becoming the possessors of a work of art of so high a standard of conception and workmanship'. The War Memorial Committee wrote they regarded the memorial to be a worthy tribute to the city's fallen and thought it would become world famous. They added their appreciation was enhanced by it being the work of an Exeter man.[326]

## The Devonshire Regiment: Exeter Cathedral and James Stevenson

Exeter has a second impressive figurative monument by another leading national artist. The Devonshire Regiment

157

105. *The Devonshire Regiment memorial in Exeter Cathedral. Its situation is constrained within the chapel.*

106. *The watchful pose as described by 'Myrander'.*

*107. The soldier was depicted as in a defensive posture.*

chose the Cathedral for its memorial possibly because it was the most prestigious church building to house it. There were precedents for doing so. A visitor today to the cathedral sees a great collection of war memorials. Amongst the many personal memorials to individuals who over the centuries have fought in war is a brass tablet to Captain Allan Peebles of the Devonshire Regiment who fought in India in 1895 and there

159

108. *Stevenson chose to represent the
soldier as muscular and wounded.*

are others dedicated to collective military service. Five of them are of particular interest.

First, in the North Transept is the striking memorial to the men of the 20th or East Devonshire Regiment who fell in the Crimean War in 1854 and 1855. It was erected in 1857 with a marble plaque giving the names of the one hundred and forty-five men. The two bronze figures were cast by Baron Marochetti of London from Russian guns taken in the Crimea by the Regiment.[327] Second, there is a marble tablet to the 9th Queen's Lancers who were in India in 1869. Third, in 1860, when Cornwall was part of the diocese, there was also erected a tablet to fifteen officers of the 32nd or Cornwall Regiment Light Infantry who died on service in India. They died while defending Lucknow and Cawnpore in 1857 and unusually, the memorial is also dedicated to three of the officers' wives and one of their daughters who, along with 43 soldiers' wives and 55 children, also died. The memorial depicts a lion biting a snake.[328] Fourthly, more than one hundred men of the Second Battalion Eleventh (North Devon) Regiment who served in the Afghan campaign of 1880 to 1881 are commemorated on an impressive brass tablet. The fifth relevant memorial takes the form of red marble wall tablets with the names of local men who died in the Boer War of 1899 to 1902. Several hundred men, including of the Devonshire Regiment, are listed by name and rank and either their regiment or service in the case of the Royal Navy.

Each of these five was a precedent for the city's First World War memorials. In 1920 the first of the Cathedral's new memorials was erected. The deaths of nine men of the 1105th Battery Royal Fleet Auxiliary were marked with the unveiling of a bronze tablet on July 28 1920.[329] In the previous year the Devonshire Regiment had agreed with the cathedral authorities to erect its memorial in the building. Brigadier General Montagu Creighton Curry, who had been with the Devons at Ladysmith, was the chief organiser.

In January 1920 cathedral officials asked for a sketch of

the monument in order to see how it could be placed and by June arrangements were being made to move the tablets of Generals Buller, Kekewich and Park to make room for the new monument. That summer the regimental colours were given to the cathedral and these were placed over the waiting space.[330]

The commission had gone to James Stevenson, a sculptor then aged forty years old. He used the pseudonym 'Myrander' which was a conflation of his wife's first name (Myra) and his second name (Alexander). His bust of King George V is in the Royal Collection and that of the Arctic explorer Shackleton in New Zealand. Stevenson was based in London and his memorial was sculpted there. He had already produced a bronze eagle for a memorial in Cambridge and would, in 1922, create the figure of a kilted soldier in bronze for Dingwall in Scotland.

Exeter's newest memorial, weighing nearly a ton, arrived on the 20th of June 1921 by motor lorry. Six days later it was unveiled by Major General Sir Louis Blois. The main figure was cast in bronze on a plinth of Italian marble. The work cost a little more than £1,100.[331] *The Western Times* thought the soldier's face conveyed 'unshakeable determination, superb self-reliance, disregard of danger'. Moreover, the paper noted:

'the lineaments of the face have been brought out with wonderful power. The sunken cheeks indicate trying physical strain and endurance. The keen eyes, the tightly closely lips, and the expression of the entire countenance reveal unshakeable determination, a cool courage which admits of no fear, and a superb power of self-reliance. The chest is bare, and the veins of the throat and neck, standing out like whipcord, indicate that the whole frame is alert. Bare to the elbow, the right arm is bound with a bandage.'[332]

Stevenson himself told a journalist he was guided:

'by the fact that the great characteristic of the Devons, and the one of which their commanders were proud, was that, no matter what were the hardships or how tight was the corner in which they found themselves, they always *stuck it*. That I have sought to make the dominating note of the whole design.'

He attributed this idea to General Curry. Stevenson also said that he had endeavoured to portray a gallant Devon who 'tough wounded, and almost knocked out, is yet sticking it, alone in an isolated spot, cool, determined and fearless'. The background was intended to represent a French battlefield and was:

'one of those devastated spots in which the Devons so often found themselves, and in which they suffered so terribly. There are indications in the distance of tree stumps, which shells have deprived of all the branches, of debris scattered all about the spot where the solider is keeping watch; of mud, and of burning homes.'

He also added that on the left of the memorial:

'the crucifix, on which is the figure of the Saviour, is in the distance from which the soldier has come. Crucifixes are typical of France, and in this instance the crucifix is symbolic of the source of the strength and power of the soldier figure in the foreground'.[333]

There does not seem to have been any controversy over this particular crucifix.

From Gibraltar Raymond Heywood, an established poet,[334] sent a poem for the unveiling of the new monument.

'The shadows softly fall where they are sleeping,
    The moonbeams dance.
Upon their beds, and they are in God's keeping –
    Somewhere in France.

109. *The Great War memorial to the Royal North Devon Hussars in
St Peter and St Paul's church in Barnstaple also features
a female figure, possibly Victory.*

Upon their graves the crimson poppies glory,
   And cornflowers, too;
White lilies to complete the floral story-
   Red, white and blue.

For Devon they died... no clarion calls were blended
   Nor lifted lance
For each small share – but just a journey ended-
   Somewhere in France.'[335]

Fifteen years later St Edmund's Chapel was re-dedicated to serve as the Devonshire Regiment's Chapel and the memorial was moved from its position on the north wall of the nave near that of the Lancers.[336] Stevenson's work can now be seen in the chapel along with a supplementary collection of other war memorials including a tablet to the Royal 1st Devon Yeomanry which was not erected until 1924.[337]

## Church embellishments

Many hundreds of war memorials were created as enhancements to religious buildings. These include stained glass, carved wood, organs, shrines, altar crosses and chapels. One of the more unusual is that at Chudleigh Knighton. The memorial is itself the church gate and not the cross which surmounts it: at the time it was noted that parishioners coming to church would pass through the gate and thereby have a constant reminder of the war.[338] A surprising range of objects were given as war memorials. These comprise such items as an altar frontal in Barnstaple,[339] a funeral bier at Parkham, an ambry at Branscombe, an alms dish at Frithelstock, a hymn board at Culmstock, a copy of Leonardo de Vinci's The Last Supper at Bampton and a lectern at Bradworthy. Others include the bell which in 1919 was installed in the church tower at Aylesbeare to honour the death in action of the vicar's son who 'sleeps in an unknown grave but his name liveth for evermore'.[340]

A sanctuary light was presented to the Anglican church at Washford Pyne in 1920. It was not the only church to have lighting: St Matthias Church in Torquay had the installation of its electric light paid for as a war memorial. There was also a candle holder given as a war memorial to St Anne's church in Saunton. Other unusual items include the font cover presented to the parish church of Charles near Exmoor which was not the only one: another was given to the Anglican church at Dalwood in East Devon.

Stained glass windows were one of the most common of the war memorial embellishments. They were erected in both church and chapel. The Wesleyans, for example, had a war memorial window at Holsworthy[341] and the Baptists erected one at Bradninch by Arnold Robinson of the Bristol Guild of Applied Art in honour of his cousin Lieutenant Roger Hepburn.[342] Dozens of others were placed in Free Churches in all parts of Devon. Some of the stained glass schemes were ambitious in replacing great West Windows, such as at Emmanuel Church in Plymouth,[343] and for East Windows such as at Emmanuel Church in Exeter.

Local craftsmen were responsible for a high number of the war memorial windows in Devon. F. Drake & Sons of Exeter designed and executed work in such places as Bovey Tracey,[344] Cullompton,[345] Newton St Cyres,[346] Uplowman,[347] West Teignmouth[348] and St Barnabas in Dartmouth.[349] Mr H. Blanchford of Exeter was responsible for war memorial windows across Devon including at Pilton[350] and Teigngrace.[351]

The Drake firm is responsible for creating some of the most striking Great War memorial stained glass. That at Bampton is perhaps one of the most unusual in Devon as a war memorial. The window includes fragments of fifteenth-century glass which was restored by Maurice Drake of Exeter. It was removed from a window behind the organ and unveiled as a war memorial in 1921.[352] Three of the firm's other commissions are more representative.

These Drake windows at West Teignmouth, Newton St

110. *The gate to Chudleigh Knighton.*

Cyres and Bovey Tracey have a common feature: the men are recorded in the panes of glass together with their regimental and naval badges. West Teignmouth's glass lists 111 men and has the four patron saints of England, Wales, Scotland and Ireland. Drake had a gallery removed in order to install the glass. That window cost some four hundred pounds and was

167

111. *Three individuals were depicted with great accuracy in stained glass memorial windows. One of them is Cecil Whitaker of Broadclyst.*

112. *The second individual for whom there is a striking likeness in stained glass is Ruth Whittaker, a VAD nurse.*

113. *The third person in the stained glass window is a second sister, Ursula Whittaker.*

unveiled in 1920. He noted that the diagonal panes were an English design in stained glass.[353] Two years later the glass window was completed at Bovey Tracey. Maurice Drake was again the craftsman. His design features four French and English 'soldier saints'; the figures are St Martin of Tours, St Oswald, King Alfred and St Joan of Arc. Drake's intention was to depict the spiritual forces that that 'animated the nation in prosecuting the war and through God brought it to victory'. King Alfred was depicted with a book on a Danish longship, partly to show this ship of his own design as the nucleus of the British navy but also to illustrate the suggested initial British motive in the war which was the defence of the weak. St Oswald is depicted striking a cross into the ground before leading his army against the heathens. He represents the later British motive in the war which was the defence of 'our own freedom and existence'. The two French saints are there as England's greatest ally. St Joan represents patriotism and St Martin is shown dividing his cloak to symbolise the self-sacrifice of Bovey's fallen heroes. The fifty-five men local men being honoured are noted by their initials, service badge and date of death.[354]

The window at Newton St Cyres is different to the others in that it was created to mainly commemorate Captain Edward Owen St Cyres Godolphin Quicke, the lay rector of the parish. He died in the first months of the war. The glass depicts three Old Testament Warriors and an angel: they are Joshua, St Michael the Archangel, David and Jonathan. Four battle-themed roundels within wreaths appear beneath them illustrating Moses praying for victory over Amalek, St Michael overpowering the dragon, David going out against Goliath and Jonathan smiting the Philistines. Throughout the window are the names of the nineteen local men who died along with their military badges. The window was unveiled in 1920.[355]

Some of the stained glass pictorially alludes to the fallen. At Withycombe Raleigh the vicar memorialised his two sons who died in the war. It was noted at the time that the 'design is exquisitely appropriate in its symbolism, representing as it does not only the idea of brotherhood but also the sharing of Christ's cup of sacrifice'. Included in the window were the figures of the 'brother knights', Sir Galahad and Sir Percival. It was said to illustrate 'the beauty of sorrow and sacrifice'.[356] A year later a second window was installed in the church: it depicts Christ offering the Crown of Life to a kneeling soldier. A brass tablet lists the names of all 131 local men who died in the war.[357] In the Methodist Church in Sidwell Street in Exeter are two stained glass war memorials. One of them is to a twenty-three year old lieutenant who died at Ypres in 1917. His window depicts David, as a man carrying his sling, while in the background can be seen Goliath and his men marching towards him.

At Chulmleigh church there is a memorial window to Margaret Hanson who died while a VAD nurse at the age of 23. The window, placed in a window which was near her grave, notes 'her joyous life was laid down on the 9th of May 1917 in the service of God and country'. It was executed by Mr Blanchford of Exeter.[358] Miss Hanson was not included in the list of those honoured in the town war memorial cross. Broadclyst also has an interesting window. It overshadows the nearby parish war memorial window which is itself highly accomplished, with its figures of Victory and Hope along with a soldier kneeling before Jesus, but the second window is exceptionally particular to the village. The window was erected by the vicar to his son, Captain Cecil Whitaker, who was killed in 1916 at the age of twenty-nine. He is depicted in the window along with his sisters Ursula and Ruth, both of whom were V.A.D. nurses.[359]

One of the finest of the war memorials was erected at Ringmore in the South Hams. It was unveiled in 1919 and was the work of Beatrice Campbell, an accomplished Irish-born artist who worked in stained glass in London. The window depicts St George kneeling at a wayside crucifix with a French battle scene in the background. Other details include the battle-cruiser *Queen Mary*, an anti-aircraft gun and airplane.[360] Pyworthy also has contemporary features: a plane, air-ship and battle cruiser all feature in the window glass.

The Anglican church at Leusdon at Ponsworthy on Dartmoor has an extraordinary stained glass war memorial window to Lieutenant William Torquill Macleod Bolitho who died in 1915 at the second battle of Yrpes. The window is the work of Arthur Anselm Orr, a noted stained glass artist. It represents Bolitho as Sir Galahad and among the rich details is a depiction of where Bolitho died. Equally detailed is a window at Shebbear to James William Prior Ponsford who died in France on 25 October 1916. It depicts Saints Michael, George and Gabriel.

Carved wood was one of the other main embellishments and took such form as screens, panelling and pulpits. These were often provided by individual donors to honour the memory of loved ones but occasionally money was also raised by the general public. The panelling at Holy Trinity in Exmouth is among the most impressive. It runs through the church and carries the names of the local men who died. Herbert Read of Exeter designed and carved the panels.[361]

Memorial screens were given to a number of Devon churches. In 1920 a new screen, of Devon oak, was unveiled at Woodbury. It features an angel bearing 'the palm of victory and the symbol of prayer'. The screen was carved in part or possibly in its entirety by J. B. Hunt of Plymouth to a design by Harbottle Reed, an Exeter architect.[362] Another chancel screen was erected at Sandford and, like many others, on it was carved the names of the parishioners who died in the war.[363] Tiverton also had a new oak screen: St Peter's Church acquired a considerable work carved by Herbert Read from a design by Sidney Greenslade.[364] Screens were not always carved from wood; one of iron and brass was unveiled at Budleigh Salterton's Anglican church in 1920. It was designed by G. H. Fellowes Prynne, the architect of the church which

114. *Detail of St George from the War memorial of the church of St Sidwell which was heavily bombed in the second world war. The work is probably that of Herbert Read and was erected in 1921.*

172

had been erected twenty-seven years before. It was executed by Marshal of Cheltenham.[365] Unfortunately the screen was destroyed by bombing during the Second World War.

Occasionally other embellishments were given along with a screen. This happened at Sandford which not only had a new chancel screen but choir stalls. Like nearly every other church embellishment, there was a personal tie: the stalls were in memory of Thomas Norrish, who died on the Somme, by his father.[366] John Northcott, architectural carver, was responsible for a range of embellishments in the Anglican church at Stokeinteignhead near Teignmouth. This included a carved oak shelf, tablet, pulpit, choir stalls and reredos as well as the panelling. Northcott lived in the small village of Ashwater near Holsworthy and was an unlikely choice to carve for the south Devon parish. He was not as well-known as the major firms of Harry Hems or Herbert Read but, as he pointed out, his costs were lower and it was suggested that his work was better. His profile may not have been very high even in his own village. On one occasion he had to ask his Stokeinteignhead liaison to address envelopes to him as John Northcott, carver. He explained:

'will you put carver as there is several other Northcotts in Ashwater but I am the only carver & then I am sure to receive it. This letter by this morning's post went to Mr Northcott the wheelwright first as he is the older and its always the rule to deliver to the oldest of the same name first if there is a doubt and he is called John Northcott same as me.'[367]

The gift of a new reredos was unusual but it occurred in a number of Devon churches including at Doddiscombesleigh which, like many others, was dedicated to a family member that died in the war. Others can be found in Dartmouth, Hartland and Torquay.

An unusual wooden embellishment is at Woodbury Salterton. It has a lych-gate as a memorial. It was built of oak

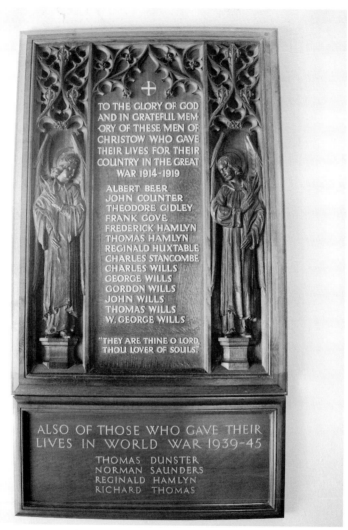

115. *Three-panelled carved wooden memorial,
with two angels, at Christow.*

116. *The Dartmouth church of St Petrox alongside the castle has carved wooden panels with lettering on the men who died during the war.*

to a Gothic design and commemorated the loss of two local men and as a thank offering to the return of the 47 other men who returned home. The gate was designed by a local man, George Bevis of Exmouth, and executed by a local firm, Jarman Brothers of Woodbury.[368] Others can be seen at Gittisham, St Mary's Roman Catholic Church in Buckfast, Feniton and West Putford.

Along with its new screen, Woodbury also had a war memorial organ. It was built by Brindley & Foster of Sheffield.[369] Crediton's organ was one of its three significant memorials to the war. In 1921 it was installed and cost some five thousand pounds. At the unveiling the organist played German music and this was deplored by a writer to the local paper that week. An ex-serviceman thought it inappropriate but another writer thought that the time had come to forgive the Germans and move forward.[370] A separate wall tablet was erected to honour Harold Organ who had been the church organist and who died in France in 1917. The tablet copied a letter from a fellow officer to his widow:

'I think he was one of the bravest men I have met out here. On one occasion after losing two of his men in a night attack he went out unaccompanied and I believe unarmed except with a Verey pistol in daylight and when we expostulated at what we thought his temerity, he told us that he could not rest until he had done all he could to find his lost men'.

Other organs were also erected including in 1919 at Holy Trinity Church in Barnstaple which had a choir organ dedicated to the twelve parishioners who died in the war.[371]

In addition to the afore-mentioned clock tower at Shaldon there were memorial clocks placed on church towers.[372] One such clock was installed in the tower of the parish church of Coldridge in 1919. It was built by Gillett and Johnson of Croydon.[373] A clock was proposed but turned down at Uplowman and one resident complained in a subsequent parish meeting that the vicar had overstated its cost. It was apparent the vicar did not want a clock in his tower: he argued few residents would be able to see it.[374] Other proposals to erect clocks were successful at Ermington, Langtree,[375] Marldon,[376] and Georgeham.[377] At Sandford the committee decided to change their existing clock and employed a man from Exeter St Thomas to install a new one.[378]

Unlike that at Halberton, a number of churches dedicated side chapels as war memorials including Peverell in Plymouth. One of the most elaborate is at Chagford which was re-dedicated in 1919. The impetus for this may have been the loss of the former rector's son; he had died in action two years earlier and the altar cross was given in his memory. The chapel's furnishings were designed by Herbert Read and included oak panelling with images of the patron saints of England, Scotland, Wales & Ireland.[379] Another was dedicated to the war at Emmanuel Church at Mannamead in Plymouth. In 1919 a carved oak screen and fittings were provided by the parents of two men who had died in action.[380]

Two Devon churches have outstanding altar crosses. One

117. *Topsham's memorial cross brought back from France and made from parts from a tank.*

is in the parish church of Topsham where its most distinctive war commemoration involved the dedication of a chapel in the church. On the 8th of October 1919 permission was sought to convert a side chapel 'as an act of Thanksgiving' for the lives of those men who had been spared and to commemorate those who had died in the war. On the 20th of July 1920 the Dean of Exeter dedicated the chapel. He said that 'the best thing in all the war was the answer of those that offered themselves willingly among the people'.[381] The church's terrier, the official listing of its possessions, later noted that:

'a copper cross and two copper flower vases in the Lady Chapel have the following history. They were designed, cut out and embossed by the Reverend Guy Halliday, then, in the autumn of 1918 serving as Chaplain to the forces, attached to the Tank Corps at Erin, Pas de Calais. The copper was from a tank radiator and the bosses on the vases are as they were on the original copper sheet. The cross was mounted over oak and made in two parts for transport. This and the vases were most skillfully soldered by a Chinaman attached to the Chinese Labour Corps.'

The church records also include a small notebook, entitled 'For the Padre', which was once kept under that cross. It is a record of donations made by men in the canteen of the Central Tank Corps Workshops at Erin during the war. They had 'sent their gift, which gift actually started the effort to provide the Lady Chapel as it now is'. The men gave 280 shillings to the vicar.[382]

At Horwood, located between Bideford and Barnstaple, is the most unusual altar cross. This crucifix was brought by a local man from Arras in 1918 and was made partly from bullets and a shell casing. It was the gift of Lieutenant Colonel Humphrey Dene, the son of Reverend John Dene of Horwood. Other altar crosses include a processional cross given in memory of two men who died from Ringmore.[383]

118. *Horwood's cross fashioned
from military armaments.*

Perhaps one of the more unusual embellishment memorials was the triptych shrine. A number of Devon churches acquired these and they served the same purpose as a community wall tablet. They took the form of a wooden niche, in three panels, featuring a saint, often with a canopy, and doors. That at Berry Pomeroy is on a niche and stands nine feet high. It has the figure of Saint George and the carving includes the name of the dead of the parish. Herbert Read was responsible for Berry Pomeroy's shrine and based his figure on the life-sized statue of St George he had carved which was previously shown in the North porch of Exeter Cathedral as part of a group of the patron saints of the Allies.[384] Earlier that year Read carved a similar shrine for Kenton.[385] There are others at Fremington, Noss Mayo, Bovey Tracey and Northam.[386]

# SIX

# CEMETERIES

Cemeteries also became war memorials. In May 1917 a cemetery war shrine, the first of its kind in the West Country, was unveiled in Exeter. It took the form of an alabaster cross, engraved with the initials IHS, on a dark oak base. There was also a roll of honour of the some sixty sailors and soldiers who had already died. The Bishop of Crediton, who had lost two sons in the war, dedicated the memorial. He said that:

> 'we, who might live in the future in a new, a better, and a happier, and he trusted, a less sinful world, would ever bear in mind that we owed it to those brave men whose bodies lay around them, and to the men who had given up all that they loved in life – their homes, their positions in life and even life itself – for the glory of a great cause.'

It was erected in the midst of the existing graves of the men who had died of war wounds in ground set aside for war heroes.[387]

Exeter, like many other places, apportioned an area in its cemetery for those men who had died in one of the many hospitals for the wounded. One journalist later recalled that

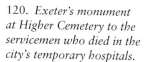

119. *A temporary cross from France incorporated into a wall tablet at Holne.*

120. *Exeter's monument at Higher Cemetery to the servicemen who died in the city's temporary hospitals.*

the city, also like many others across the country, had become accustomed to the spectacle of military funerals. He wrote:

'One stood bareheaded and watched the cortege pass with a feeling of sorrow akin to nausea that a war which caused the deaths of our young men should have ever been allowed to happen. In Exeter we saw many of such sights, no less than 188 of Britain's best were carried to a last resting place in the Higher Cemetery and were laid to rest side by side on a site specially chosen'.[388]

Three years later the City Architect designed a replacement cross, now called a Memorial.[389] Staff shortages were responsible for a lengthy delay:[390] it was not until 1922 that the cross was finally replaced. This grey Devon granite cross was a monument only to those who had died in the city: the 188 men included 12 from Australian, New Zealand and Canadian regiments. Their names were engraved on bronze tablets and around the memorial were granite blocks bearing the individual names of each man.

The cross was unveiled by the Mayor and dedicated by the Bishop. The mayor said that when the Red Cross hospitals were opened the council had undertaken to inter men who died from their wounds. The number of deaths had exceeded expectations and their graves had spilled over from what had been the intended ground. The bishop spoke of the men's sacrifices and noted many were already questioning whether it was right that these men had died. He argued it was necessary in order to build a 'truly newer and happier world'.[391] The cross cost the council £1,181 although more than two hundred pounds had been saved due to a fall in wages and in the costs of materials.[392] Torquay was another Devon place which erected a granite cross to those who died from wounds in hospitals. It was unveiled in 1922.[393]

First World War graveyard memorials to Devon men can also be found outside Britain. In November 1918 the Durban

121. *The grave of Fred Adams at Stoke Gabriel which features his bronze penny medallion.*

122. *Two of the medallions were used at Culmstock as part of a war memorial.*

*A detail of the medieval glass restored at Bampton as a war memorial.*

The names of the West Teignmouth men who died in the war are commemorated in the Anglican church in West Teignmouth.

The Bovey Tracey war memorial glass includes King Alfred.

*The stained glass memorial window at Newton St Cyres*
*features roundels of biblical scenes.*

*Another of the military scenes taken from the bible which appears in the Newton St Cyres stained glass.*

*St George is a common figure in war memorial stained glass such as in this parish memorial window at Broadclyst.*

*Christopher and Ruth Whittaker as depicted in the*
*stained glass window at Broadclyst.*

*The second sister, Ursula, in the window at Broadclyst.*

*A detail of the extraordinary window at Ringmore in the South Hams.*

*St George with an anti-aircraft gun in the background.*

*A detail showing the* Queen Mary.

*The crucifix which was a common sight in France but its depiction
in war memorials in Devon could be controversial.*

*A detail showing the men in the trenches.*

*A detail of the Ringmore window showing an airplane flying
over what appears to be the white cliffs of Dover.*

*Detail of St Adrian from Pyworthy's stained glass window to the war*
*which also features St Nicholas as the patron saint of sailors and soldiers.*
*It was unveiled in 1920 and is the work of F. Drake & Sons of Exeter.*
*St Adrian also has a tank while St Nicholas is holding a battle cruiser.*

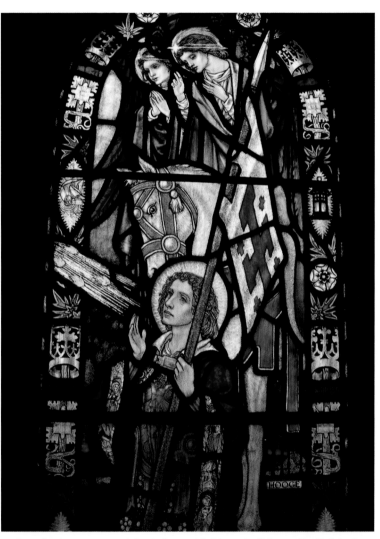

*Leusdon's war memorial window with Lieut. Bolitho as Sir Galahad.*

*Bolitho died at the second battle of Ypres on 24 May 1915.*

*Chateau Hooge, where Bolitho died, is also depicted.*

SPARE US GOOD LORD

*The memorial window at Shebbear to James William Prior Ponsford who died in France on 25 October 1916. Beside the angel surveying the chaos can be seen an airplane.*

*The two angels bringing peace in the window at Shebbear are shown above the earth over France where Ponsford died.*

Cornwall and Devon Association erected a monument in Durban to all the Westcountry soldiers and sailors who died in the Great War. It was made of African stone 'shaped after the tradition of Cornwall and Devon'.[394] A monument was also erected in Bavaria to honour the 36 prisoners of war who died in a camp in Klosterlechfeld. It was through the efforts of an Exeter man, E. May of 5 Elton Road, that the monument was created. He had been taken prisoner by the Germans in July 1917 and was President of the British Help Committee while in the camp. The prisoners themselves paid for the monument, an eight-foot high marble cross which was placed on Swiss stone.[395]

The grandest was the Devon Regimental memorial in France. It was made in Exeter by Harry Hems & Sons and exhibited in the city in May 1921 before being transported to the Continent.[396] The memorial was a rough-hewn cross, made of Dartmoor granite, and it weighed four and a half tons. It was erected at Boise de Buttes, the site of one of the regiment's most important battles. On May 27th 1918 the Second Battalion Devonshire Regiment had fought off a major German attack for which they received the *Croix de Guerre*.

On one side of the base of the granite cross was a quotation from the French Army Order of the Day. It has another inscription on two of the other sides: one is in French and the other is in English.

*2nd Battalion Devonshire Regiment*
*On the 27th May 1918 at a time when the British trenches were being subjected to fierce attacks, the 2nd Battalion Devonshire Regiment repelled successive enemy assaults with gallantry and determination and maintained an unbroken front till a late hour. The staunchness of this battalion permitted defenses south of the Aisne to be reorganized and their occupation by reinforcements to be completed. Inspired by the sangfroid of their gallant commander Lt Col. R. H. Anderson-Morshead D.S.O. in the face of intense bombardment, the few survivors of*

*the battalion, though isolated and without hope of assistance, held onto their trenches north of the river and fought to the last with an unhesitating obedience to orders. Thus, the whole battalion, 28 officers and 552 non-commissioned officers and men, responded with one accord and offered their lives in ungrudging sacrifice to the sacred cause of the allies.*

On Sunday, November 6th 1921, General Berthelot, former Commander of the French 5th Army, unveiled the memorial. He said:

'In the name of the French Army, I express our admiration for the British troops who fought by our side during the war, who submitted cheerfully to all the hardships of the campaign and whose smiling men went to death, or glory, and heroic self-sacrifice. But in particular I wish to pay special tribute to the men of the Devonshire Regiment – men I knew during one of the severest fights of the war. This ground will ever be hallowed by reason of their heroism on May 27th 1918. The men of the Devons disputed every inch of the ground. Their bravery and tenacity kept the enemy in check until we could bring up reinforcements.'[397]

There are many other cemetery memorials. The most prominent are the Imperial War Graves Commission crosses which were erected in such places as Exeter, Plymouth and Torquay. Graveyards across Devon have private gravestone. One at Halberton records the death on December 5th 1918 of Lieut. Clement Edwards, aged 20, of whom it notes 'not on the battlefield, yet none the less, he died for England'. A few of them, such as one at Stoke Gabriel, have placed on them the bronze penny medallions, commonly called the 'dead man's penny', which were given to the next of kin mark the deaths of the men. Across the country Devon men are remembered on other memorials in places in which they worked or later lived.

# SEVEN

# THE UNVEILING OF COMMUNITY MEMORIALS

The community memorials were almost always unveiled with great fanfare. That at Buckfastleigh was revealed after the town band had marched to the church along with one hundred soldiers. A great crowd watched the ceremony which involved Anglican, Wesleyan and Congregational clergy.[398] The war memorials were usually unveiled by a local worthy who was often a military man, politician or a member of the local gentry. In only a few instances was a serviceman from the rank and file called upon to unveil the monument. This happened at Sticklepath when the cross was unveiled by Private James Wright. He was the oldest soldier present. It also happened at Welcombe along the north Cornish border but few soldiers were given the honour unless they were senior men. At Instow Private John Barrett was asked only because Major General Sir L. S. Bois was unable to attend. There were reasons to ask Barrett: he had lost one leg whilst serving his country and his brother was listed on the memorial.[399] The crowds could be very large. Those at Tavistock and Teignmouth were said to have stood at two thousand[400] while at Exeter there were some 50,000 people. Plymouth had many more.[401] At Brixton

123. *The unveiling of Uplyme's memorial, 1920.*

nearly every resident turned out for the unveiling and after the vicar proclaimed 'I unveil this cross to the glory of God and in memory of the men of Brixton who gave their lives in the country's cause' there was a long silence punctuated only by the sobbing of the bereaved.[402] Perhaps the most disappointing unveiling took place at Northam. Its statue of liberty, similar to that in New York but certainly not a replica, was delayed with the result that only the pedestal could be unveiled. The ceremony had to take place because of the imminent holiday of the chairman of the local council. The statue arrived shortly afterwards.[403] Local politics and rivalries were played out in the unveiling of war memorials including in the small village of Germansweek where one speaker used the unveiling to attack trade unions.[404]

After the unveiling the memorial was dedicated by a

124. *Crediton's unveiling of the civic memorial with a background more open than today.*

125. *The unveiling of the monument for the city of Plymouth attracted a considerable crowd.*

189

churchman. The Bishops of Exeter and Crediton were often called upon for this duty and these must have been bitter-sweet experiences for them as they each had lost children in the war. Three of Bishop Cecil's four sons died in the war and Bishop Trefusis lost two of his four sons.[405] The dedication given by the Dean of Exeter at Branscombe provides a sense of what society expected to hear at such events. He said:

'There was nothing else in all the world to equal the first great response that came from the men who went out willingly to offer themselves. Of all kinds and all classes, landlords, farmers, labourers, artisans, clerks, scholars, most of them lovers of peace, they were not anxious to enter upon the ways of war, and yet, when the great need arose, and the question came to them, they were ready to answer "Here am I, send me". No doubt, amongst the earliest men to answer the call were some of those whose memory they commemorated that day. They went out, but they did not return, and their names, as they know, were written far away in Egypt, in Gallipoli, in Mesopotamia, and the stricken fields of Flanders and France. There they won their fame, and though their bodies lay in graves, far away their souls were marching on.'[406]

The unveilings, and the Armistice Day commemorations which took place in the early 1920s, were conducted with a large contingent of the bereaved. These were not only family and friends who had been left behind but ex-servicemen, many of whom had shared experiences with the dead in battle including witnessing their deaths. It is likely that these bonds were stronger in small villages where so many monuments were raised. One purpose of the unveilings was to offer consolation to the bereaved and to adequately honour the dead. The unveilings provided an opportunity for communities, through their speakers, to express appreciation for the service of those who had gone abroad and to reassure the bereaved that the losses were regarded with honour and that they were not in

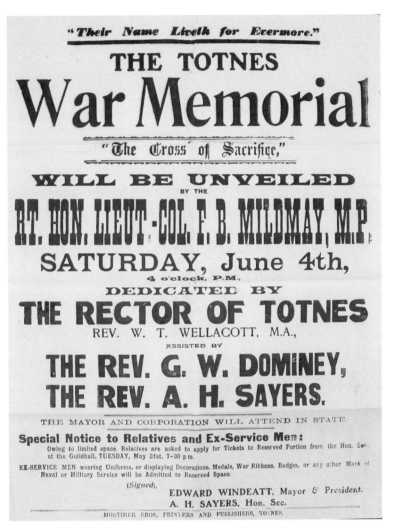

*126. Announcement of the unveiling at Totnes.*

vain. The bishop told the crowd at Barnstaple that they had to ask themselves what did the men die for? His answer was the world would have been dominated by Germany and the powers of evil. Whereas Germany was the tool of the devil in

## SPECIAL
# Notice to Relatives & Ex-Service Men.

## Totnes War Memorial Unveiling Ceremony
### SATURDAY, JUNE 4TH, 4 O'CLOCK, P.M.

**All Relatives and Ex-Service Men are requested to enter by the North Gate (opposite Guildhall), and to be in their places not later than 3.45.**

**EDWARD WINDEATT,**
*Mayor and President.*

**A. H. SAYERS,**
*Hon. Sec.*

Mortimer Bros., Printers and Publishers, Totnes.

127. *The guidance leaflet for relatives and former servicemen at Totnes.*

contrast he felt that behind England was 'some great mysterious spiritual power'.[407] At Berry Pomeroy the local vicar told his crowd that 231 years previously a foreign army had marched through the parish, that of William of Orange, but his army had come to deliver England from an unconstitutional monarch. In contrast, how differently, he said, would it have been if a German army had been in Devon. Their boys had saved them from an 'unspeakable horror'.[408]

Some speakers used the unveilings to tell the audience why the men fought. Paymaster Commander Andrews, chairman of the war memorial committee at Plympton St Maurice, told the crowd in 1924 that:

'We must recognise the human motives which caused these men to take their part in the war. One great thing in their minds through it all – parents, wife, children, home and you

– and the determination to prevent the enemy harming you either by invasion, blockade or starvation. That determination saved the country and us – it cost them their lives.'[409]

It was also a time in which audiences could be reminded of what the fighting entailed. Colonel C. R. Burn, the Conservative M. P. for Torquay who would become one of the country's first and most prominent fascists only two years later,[410] said at the unveiling of Paignton's memorial 'to the known horrors of war horrors altogether unknown were added. The resources of science were put to strange and barbarous uses by land and sea and air.' Burns himself lost a son in the war and had travelled to France in an attempt to find his grave.[411]

More detailed were the comments by Colonel Francis Mildmay, Liberal M.P. for Totnes and later First Baron Mildmay of Flete, who told the crowd at the unveiling of Teignmouth's memorial he doubted they could understand what the men had gone through and hesitated to express his thoughts as he held his own memories as sacred. Mildmay spoke of the fighting of the second battle at Ypres where the conditions were 'truly desperate'. He also talked of when the Germans first used poison gas.

'A faint odour drifted across their position. I could almost smell it now. They sniffed and they sniffed – what was it? In later days they did not stop to sniff. The meaning of it soon became apparent, for the French black colonial troops poured past them in a rushing retreat, terrified, their eyes staring out of their heads, tearing at their throats, devoured by the gas, they thought they were possessed by the devil. British troops were rushed up to fill the gap, many of them Territorials. With no gas masks, it was necessary to meet the devilish poison. They did it, and repelled the Germans – but at what cost?'

Mildmay also spoke of the fighting of the Somme.

'There the British had carried on the fighting far into the winter, they had sacrificed themselves to help the French. In those days the men would have been rightly described as living almost under water, up to their eyes in half frozen filth, morning and night, never dry. The whole country on the Somme front was pitted with enormous shell holes, full to the brim with liquid mud, of the consistency of glue. Many men and horses had been engulfed therein whilst struggling forward. So insistent and ever present was the danger that, in certain parts, every third man of a relieving unit carried a rope for life-saving purposes'.

Some of the men were so imbedded in the mud that it took hours to set them free.[412] The unveiling was also a time to assert that the memorial was intended to last for generations. The Earl of Iddesleigh said at Upton Pyne that:

'They might hope that as long as Upton Pyne was a parish inhabited by English men and women that cross would preserve the names inscribed on it and that generation after generation would do honour to these heroes.'[413]

The unveilings were intended to crystallise the message of the monuments and launch them into the life of the community.

# EIGHT

# THE CONTROVERSY OVER INAPPROPRIATE CRUCIFIXES

War memorials were occasionally contentious when they opened up religious differences. Some parishes in the diocese of Exeter then had a reputation for leaning towards the High Church and frictions occurred in some of those urban churches, in Torbay, Exeter and Plymouth, which were higher than most. The issue was of particular concern in the resort of Paignton through 1919. One of the proposals for a community monument was for a Calvary Cross, which is a Latin cross placed on three steps. The vicar of Christ Church, a newly-built Anglican church in the town, wrote with some uncompromising determination to the committee about this option:

'A Calvary being representative of the pagan Roman method of the capital punishment of malefactors would be in a Christian community a contravention of the 39th Article of religion to which clergymen of the Church of England were pledged. It would be illegal if erected inside a consecrated Church of England, a breach of the Second Commandment and as such an offence to bible Christians, who form an overwhelming majority of the community, and a stumbling block to the Jews, whose treatment of our enemies and loyalty to us and our Allies during the war deserved better from us than what would be tantamount to a public insult.'[414]

His opposition to a Calvary Cross would have surprised some Devonians at the time but not so much had it been a Crucifix which was controversial. There were many supporters of them for war memorials. One former serviceman wrote that after witnessing the 'pain, torture and unmerited death' whilst fighting in France he found the sight of a wayside crucifix still standing amidst 'devastating hell-fires' inspirational. He could not understand the reluctance to allow crucifixes on war memorials[415] but another resident said he and others were astonished by the vicar's reasoning and saddened that the committee felt because of the controversy that they were unable to put up a monument with any Christian symbols so therefore decided upon an obelisk, which in his mind was pagan.[416] Paignton had also seen controversy over the use of a cross for an outdoor memorial service. Demobilised servicemen had organised a public service for the community to show its gratitude towards them but the servicemen refused to hold it in a religious building on the grounds that it would limit numbers and they wanted to keep it nondenominational. A temporary cenotaph was erected in the centre of the town and the Roman Catholics placed a plain wooden cross along the seafront. The *Churchman's Magazine* complained of what they saw as collusion on behalf of the Anglicans and Nonconformists in promoting idolatory.[417] The result was a community monument which one committee member suggested was incapable of causing offence, an obelisk.[418]

Other types of controversies regarding Anglican doctrine occurred in other parts of Devon. It was claimed elsewhere in 1920 that a Wesleyan minister had asked the public for prayers for the dead but he wrote to a newspaper to point out this was not his comment but one made by the Anglican

128. *An early war shrine at St Peter's Church, Plymouth. On the left is the list of men of the parish then serving in the war and on the right a framed picture of a crucified Jesus appearing to a dying soldier.*

129. *The second street shrine at St Olave's church in Exeter.*

cleric.[419] Two years later the Bishop of Exeter refused to allow the rector of the Dartmoor parish of Belstone permission to erect a bronze statue of Christ on the exterior of the church. The cleric had another war memorial which were figures on the rood screen.[420] The proposed erection of crucifixes was the issue which caused greatest controversy in Anglican churches across Devon. At a public meeting in Dartmouth in 1919 one speaker said the proposed idea of a crucifix was one which was repulsive to many in the port.[421] Even so they were erected in several places but not always peacefully. Two in Devon aroused particular controversy. An ancient church in Exeter was the first.

On January 10th 1917 the Bishop of Crediton dedicated a street 'war shrine' in St Olave's church. This small church became the focus of an uproar which went beyond Exeter. The *Express & Echo* had reported the unveiling in a nonchalant manner.

'The first war shrine to be erected in Exeter, and, it is believed the second in Devon, was dedicated at St Olave's Church yesterday by the Lord Bishop of Crediton (Canon Trefusis). The idea of providing a shrine originated with the respected rector of the parish, Rev. E. C. Long, who had seen many on the continent, and had been impressed by their usefulness to people who used them devotionally. His parishioners generously supported the project and a disused and blocked-up doorway in the south wall of the church, immediately abutting to the main street, provided a very convenient site. It is hoped to be able to erect a number of other shrines in the streets of the parish. There are over a hundred names on the St Olave Roll of Honour which is confined to parishioners who are worshippers at the church. Of these, eight have given their lives. The shrine itself is a beautiful piece of work. The old doorway is filled in with fumed English oak, heavily moulded round the ridge at the top. There is a full-length cross of wainscot oak, with Calvary steps, the whole surmounted with a piece of black English oak cut from a beam over 500 years old, and bearing an oxidised crucifix. 'Pray for the men of St. Olaves' is the inscription in gold letters. A shelf is provided for flowers. The Roll of Honour is contained in two frames, one being for the fallen.'[422]

The shrine was placed on the exterior of the building. The Bishop expressed the hope that the shrine would make passers-by pause and think of those in whose memory it had been dedicated and consider the greater and higher things that awaited them in the next world.[423]

Letters began to appear in local newspapers immediately after this report and a heated debate ensued over whether it was appropriate for churches to erect such memorials. Concerns were voiced that they were being worshiped as idols and that the shrines encouraged prayers for the dead: in effect, it was argued, Anglican churches were being used for Catholic practices. One writer countered that the shrine was not different from any previous memorial but that the word itself was an innovation and was being objected to solely because of assumed Catholic associations.[424]

The term had been used for a London church memorial and for private ones erected in Regent Square in October 1916. Both were visited by Queen Mary.[425] It is not known if other street shrines were erected in the parish of St Olave as the vicar had hoped but there were others erected later in Devon including in Paignton and Torquay.[426] St Olave's Reverend Long was High Church. He had held a Requiem Eucharist in the church weeks before he erected his street shrine. Also participating in that service were other Exeter clergy and, most interestingly, the Reverend Robert Boggis of Barnstaple who had published *Praying for the Dead*. His booklet had been approved by the Bishop of Crediton for use in the Diocese of Exeter. Boggis preached at St Olave's service and amongst his comments was the hope that the war would reintroduce into Anglican use the Orthodox and Catholic practice of prayers for the dead.[427] It was this issue that received a great deal of unfavourable comment in the letters pages of the *Express & Echo*.

The shrine at St Olaves prompted a protest visit by John Alfred Kensit, the son of the founder of the Protestant Truth Society. He, along with his Wickliffe Preachers, came to

Exeter on the 27th of February 1917 to a well-attended public meeting. Kensit called the war shrine movement despicable and calculated to turn men from religion. He also criticized the Bishop of Crediton and urged the Bishop of Exeter, then newly enthroned, to stop his clergy from using the war to introduce idolatry to the Anglican Church.[428] The following day four unidentified men and two boys visited the church and tore the carved figure of Jesus from the altar crucifix. It was suggested by one local newspaper that the damage was done inside the church, and not to the war shrine on the exterior of the church, because it was less detectable by members of the public. The rector called the act sacrilege.[429]

Nevertheless, the shrine appears to have continued in its place through the war. In the autumn of 1918, when it appeared there would be a peace treaty, the rector suggested at a vestry meeting that the time had come when the parishioners would need to reconsider their shrine. Herbert Read, the well-known Exeter sculptor, was asked to provide two designs for a replacement memorial and in April 1922 the chosen scheme was unveiled on the spot of the old war shrine.[430] It depicts Jesus on the cross with St John and St Mary on either side and was carved of Derbyshire stone. On it was inscribed 'Glory to God and Peace to the Souls of the Men of St Olaves who fell in the War 1914–1918'. Twenty-one men are listed.

At the unveiling Sir Robert Newman, the city's M.P., said he hoped that war memorials would teach future generations that brave hearts beat in men living in the twentieth century as they had in previous generations. He also approved of the subject of the memorial 'for it often struck him that some of the war memorials were very useless, teaching nothing, and standing for very little'. The depiction of Christ on a cross, he also said, was a reminder that Christ had given his life for us just as the soldiers and sailors had done. The monument remains on the street today.[431]

A second controversy began in a separate part of Devon in 1920. In September that year a wooden crucifix was

130. *Devonport's church of St Stephen's unveiling of what
became a highly controversial crucifix.*

erected on the north-east corner outside St Stephen's Church
in Devonport. One local newspaper noted it was twenty-feet
high, that it was 'an imposing and beautiful war memorial'
and that it had 'a life-sized figure of our Lord, the whole being
a very fine specimen of the carvers' art'. The Venerable E. F.

Newman, Archdeacon of Plymouth, unveiled the monument which had been carved by J. B. Hunt, sculptor, of Plymouth. Newman said that the memorial was intended to commemorate the forty men of the parish who had imitated Jesus in giving their lives for mankind. The archdeacon also said that 'surely they did devote their lives to a holy cause, the cause of their land, of freedom, liberty and honour, and the cause of the kingdom of God'.[432]

Two years earlier the parish had decided to erect a memorial at a public meeting at which the vicar suggested a crucifix. A circular was issued and the design was specified as a stone figure on a granite cross underneath which would be a panel with the soldiers' names. However, the cross which was erected was of wood, as was the figure, and the panel was not erected until a month later and it was placed on the wall of the church twelve feet away. In effect, the panel and crucifix were independent of each other.

The first intimation of controversy came shortly after the erection. A public meeting was held and it was chaired by the vicar of nearby St Paul's Church. The speaker was John Kensit who three years earlier had rallied protests against the street shrine in Exeter. He called the memorial an idol shrine and claimed that the people of Devonport were against it. Seven months later, in March 1921, the issue of the crucifix was brought before the Consistory Court. There had been no official permission to erect the monument which was on consecrated ground and the Chancellor heard evidence about the nature of the church which was said to have practices inconsistent with Anglican doctrine. It transpired that the previous Bishop of Exeter had ordered the removal of a statue of St Joseph from the church and there were accusations of superstitious practices, including the lighting of candles for prayers. It was also claimed that reverence was shown to the crucifix but the vicar claimed to have only seen one soldier salute it and two clergymen remove their hats to it. Shortly afterwards the Chancellor reached his decision. He referred

131. *The war memorial crucifix at St John the Evangelist's church in Torquay. It had been a leading church in Anglo-Catholicism since it was erected in the 1870s.*

132. *Detail of the war memorial cross at St John the Evangelist in Plymouth. The church has been regarded as Anglo-Catholic for generations.*

133. *The Great War cross at St Mary's church in Bideford.*

134. *The war memorial at Shaldon near Teignmouth which does not appear to have been as controversial as others.*

135. *Detail of the crucifix from the Devonshire Regimental monument in Exeter Cathedral which was said at the time to be representative of those the soldiers were accustomed to seeing on the battlefront.*

to the issue as 'a most unhappy story'. He had disregarded two petitions, one for and the other against, which had been presented because twenty-five people had signed both. In his opinion the parishioners had not been consulted properly, he noted that it had been thought necessary for the police to protect the crucifix and decided that there was a danger of a superstitious reverence or use to be made of the crucifix and of dissension within the parish. Because of that he ordered that the crucifix's removal and gave a month to do so in order to avoid an unseemly public struggle.[433]

The crucifix was subsequently taken down and placed into storage. St Stephen's Church itself was badly damaged by German bombing in the Second World War and subsequently demolished. During the war the building in which the crucifix was stored was bombed. According to one writer the building in which it was stored was hit by a German bomb in the Second World War and the crucifix was subsequently discovered floating Plymouth Sound.[434]

Other places in Devon erected crucifixes but they did not attract the protests that were heard in Exeter in Plymouth. Shaldon had a crucifix as a war memorial. In November 1920 a wooden crucifix was placed near the entrance to the church. It was described as 'a large oak cross with the life-size figure of the Saviour'.[435] In March 1919 Barnstaple's Mayoress reported that a group of ladies were strongly in favour of a crucifix being erected outside St Anne's Chapel because soldiers 'had seen a lot of that sort of thing in France and it was thought they would welcome it here'.[436] The church of St Peter, regarded as a high church, in Brixham also erected a crucifix. The monument, noted as a war shrine by a local newspaper, was of oak with a solid silver crucifix as the central figure. The crucifix had been presented to the previous vicar when he left Brixham and bequeathed to the church by his widow. It is now in All Saints' Church. The dedication was by Reverend Carden of Torquay who had been chaplain with the Salonika Expeditionary Field Force. He said 'all the human life of Jesus

– the life of sacrifice – was symbolised in the crucifix. That symbol was placed on the centre of the shrine. How they loved to think that that symbol was passed again and again on the road-sides in France as many brave lads went to their deaths'. [437] Other crucifixes can still be seen outside of such Anglican churches as at Bideford, St John's in Torquay and St John the Evangelist in Plymouth. Each of them, unlike that at Devonport, had been erected as war memorials but they had their war inscriptions placed at or near the cross. Each of these churches also had reputations as being High Church during the First World War and in the immediate years afterwards.

# NINE

# THE MESSAGE OF
# THE MEMORIALS:
# INSCRIPTIONS AND WREATHS

The monuments themselves, both communal and private, have messages on the remembrance of the Great War. They tell us what society at the time thought the memorials were for and what they officially wanted later generations to know. The families themselves left messages as well. A few newspaper reports noted the inscription on the wreaths: these personal messages about those that are commemorated are the only means by which we can recapture the thoughts of the bereaved.

Not surprisingly there was not a consensus on the purpose of memorials. The chairman of the Dawlish committee suggested that the town monument was not intended to remember those who lost their lives but was rather 'a memorial to an event'. He wanted a memorial that his generation, and those to come for a thousand years, would 'look at and call to mind that England in the course of her history was engaged in the most momentous war the world had ever waged, and that in the course of the war for righteousness and justice she had won through'.[438] Other men and women suggested other reasons in meetings and ceremonies across Devon. The monuments provide us, in their own words, what was agreed in order for future generations to understand the war.

The memorials themselves proclaim, publicly at the time and to all subsequent generations, what the purpose of each memorial was as well as what the war itself was about. Most were made to remember those who had died but that at Pyworthy, along the Cornish border, was 'erected and given to commemorate the safe return of the men of this parish who fought in the Great War' while at Bickleigh near Plymouth is the similar sentiment of 'also in gratitude for the safe return of others who served'. At Shaldon the monument was firstly 'to commemorate the victorious ending of the Great War' and secondly to record the memory of the local men who had died.

The inscriptions of nearly all monuments begin with the words 'to the glory of God'[439] but thereafter there follows wording which is unique to each place. The vast majority use English but occasionally there is Latin such as at Doddiscombesleigh (*Pro Patria, Pro Deo, Pro Nobis* – for Country, for God, for Us). At Shaldon an ancillary line was added 'It is sweet and right to die for your country, pray for us', a common used phrase at the time.[440] Many memorials have biblical passages while others proclaimed 'their name liveth for ever more' (Awliscombe), 'they shall not grow old' (Beer), 'they died that we might live' (Combe Martin) and 'is it nothing to you all ye that pass by?' (Exmouth). Some are particularly stirring. There are several which noted 'Live for England, we for England died' (including Buckland Monachorum) but others are more distinctive including 'These men of ours, unselfish, unafraid, went to the world-wide fight, forget not how they fought, and how we prayed, for England and the right' (Otterton) which was used on war memorials elsewhere across the country. An unusual one is at Mortehoe which has 'Their lives for their country, their souls for their God'. At Northam there is a copy of Charles Kingsley's paraphrasing of a biblical passage with

'The men were very good unto us and we were not hurt, they were a wall unto us both by night and day.' Herbert Read thought three lines were commonly used: 'their name liveth for evermore', 'death is swallowed up in victory', and 'Greater love hath no man than this'.[441]

Only a handful of memorials speak as directly to the onlooker as Lympstone does. It proclaims 'I stand to the memory of the men of Lympstone who gave their lives in the Great War, 1914–1918' while nearby at Woodbury is 'I stand to the proud and glorious memory of the men of this parish who gave their lives in the Great War'. Likewise, three monuments in the south-west corner of Dartmoor are similar: those at Shaugh Prior and Walkhampton announce 'I stand to bear proud and lasting witness' while another at Tavistock states 'I stand to bear proud witness to these men of Tavistock who died for England in the Great War'. That at Membury asks 'Bear ever in your memory the brave deeds of our soldiers from this parish who fell for England in the Great War' while that at Throwleigh it implores the reader to 'Pray for the souls of those who fell in the Great War especially Hugh Fanshawe Glanville and James Alfred Mortimore'. At Abbotsham in North Devon the cross asks 'Remember the brave men' while that at Marwood it instructs the reader 'All honour give to those who nobly striving nobly fell that we might live'.

Some are different in nearly every respect. This is the case with Chudleigh Knighton's tablet which was inscribed 'Erected with faith in God – the giver of life immortal – to the cherished memory of those men honoured and beloved in this place who fighting for the right lost their lives in the Great War 1914-18'. Lynton's is also unusual in that it was inscribed 'Remember those who at the call of our King died the noblest death men may die, fighting for God, for right, and for liberty. Such death is immortality'. Another is that at Meavy which entreats 'All ye who pass this way remember with gratitude those who gave their lives in the Great War'.

An usual inscription was composed for Tiverton's memorial library:

'War Memorial. In Thanksgiving to God for Victory and in honour of the officers and men of Tiverton who served nobly and suffered willingly during the Great War for the deathless cause of right and liberty, 1914–1919'[442]

However, the most original inscription in Devon is probably that at Noss Mayo near Plymouth. After an almost standard 'erected by friends to the memory of lives laid down whilst serving in the Great War of 1914–1918' there follows a unique statement.

'Germany started war with the cry "world domination or downfall". Our brave lads sprang to arms to defend Belgium, our Empire and the world. Through God's goodness we & our allies won victory in 1918, yet at a mighty sacrifice of life & treasure. A glorious part in that sacrifice was taken by Revelstoke lads, whose graves are afar off on land & sea'.

Community memorials located within religious buildings are more likely to have religious sentiments. One of the best examples of this is at Bovey Tracey. It was inscribed:

'Hallowed in Christ be the memory of all who for king & country & the freedom of the world gave their lives in the Great War. They shall yet stand before the throne of God, an exceeding great army and in the last great muster shall be round these our beloved'.

Some memorials note the war as the Great War and others as the European War. For some it was 'the Great European War' (Branscombe and Buckfastleigh), for another 'the Great World War' (West Alvington), and yet more simply 'the war'

(Bratton Clovelly). Only those which were erected later after 1945 note it as the First World War.

Many men and women were noted as having fought for their country or for their King and Country but for others it was 'for Britain and Honour' (Dartington), 'for God, for King, for Country' (Branscombe), 'King and Empire' (Drewsteignton), 'for King, Country and Freedom' (Lydford), 'for us' (Brent Tor), 'for God, their country and us' (St Giles-in-the-Wood), 'for their country and for humanity' (Modbury), 'for England' (Tavistock) and 'for country and home' (Upton Pyne), 'in defence of Righteousness and Freedom' (Washfield), 'in the cause of liberty and honour' (Chudleigh), 'fighting for freedom and victory' (Cullompton), 'for their country's freedom' (Culmstock), 'for home and freedom' (Dalwood), 'who died to defend our homes' (Morebath), 'for freedom and honour' (Newton Abbot), 'to save the land they loved' (Ottery St Mary), 'who served in the cause of liberty and justice' (Shebbear), 'that we might live in freedom' (South Tawton), 'for righteousness and freedom' (Zeal Monachorum), 'for justice, righteousness and the freedom of the nations' (St Boniface in Devonport) and 'in defence of their king and country' (West Alvington).[443]

The deaths are all, not surprisingly, expressed as willingly done. The memorials include men 'who fell' (Abbotskerswell), 'who sacrificed their lives' (Bishop's Nympton), 'who made the supreme sacrifice' (Bere Alston), 'who gave their lives' (Ashton), 'with noble devotion laid down their lives' (Bradninch), 'who nobly gave their lives' (Cornwood), 'who sacrificed their lives that others might live in freedom' (Broadhembury), 'who counting not their lives dear unto them died for their country' (Coldridge), 'who responded to the call of duty' (Inwardleigh) and 'who served for us and in the cause of God' (Kentisbeare).

These individuals were 'brave men' (Ashburton), 'gallant men' (Beer), 'heroes' (Colaton Raleigh), 'fallen heroes' (Buckland Brewer), 'brave sons' (Cullompton), 'brave boys' (Welcombe), 'sailors, soldiers and all men of this parish' and 'sailors, soldiers and airmen of this parish' (East Teignmouth), 'martyrs' (East Allington), 'glorious dead' (Ermington) and 'our heroic fellow citizens' (Brixham).

Many were 'to the memory of' but there were many variances including 'loving memory' (Washfield), 'in honoured memory and grateful remembrance' (Ashburton), 'in proud and grateful memory' (Beer), 'in ever grateful memory' (Kentisbeare), 'in proud and honoured memory' (Butterleigh), 'in proud, honoured and loving memory' (Kenton), 'in undying memory' (Brentor), 'in affectionate remembrance' (Chawleigh), 'in loving memory' (Dalwood), 'in perpetual memory' (Germansweek) and 'thankful memory' (Winkleigh).

Even the dates of the war differ. Many list the war as having lasted from 1914 to 1918 but for some it was 1914 to 1919. The confusion lies with the Armistice having begun in 1918 and the peace treaty being signed a year later but the date of 1919 could also allude to the continued fighting of the Devonshire Regiment in Russia that year against the Bolsheviks. Two other monuments differently date the war's end: that at West Alvington recorded 'August 1914 to November 1918', by which it meant the war ended with the truce of 1918, but that at Cornworthy interpreted the end of the war with the signing of the Peace Treaty at Versailles: it notes '4 August 1914 to 28th June 1919'.

Many do not list the men by name generally because there were either too many or because it was too costly. Some specified that the names were noted in the church (including Brampford Speke, Buckerell, Spreyton) or 'are recorded in both church and chapel' (Cornwood). At Bideford the town's cross notes the names are kept in the borough records. Some monuments noted who the memorial was for such as 'of this place and neighbourhood' (Clyst Honiton), 'connected with East Allington by birth, schooling, residence or otherwise', 'of Hennock and Teign village' and 'from this parish and district' (Butterleigh).

The memorials to individuals provide scope for more

216

imagination and individuality. One near Kingsbridge, in the Anglican church at West Alvington, was erected to the memory of Lieutenant Eric Liptrott and noted he was mortally wounded at in the trenches in France in 1914 and died five days later in Boulogne. It went on to record 'he was mentioned in dispatches in a night attack on 16th November he saved his wounded subadar's life, carrying him under heavy fire into safety'. At Bampton a tablet was placed to a Royal Flying Corps officer 'whose mortal remains lie at Le Rutoire near Loos where he gave his life for his country in the battle of 25 September 1915. His gallantry when he was partly gassed in rallying men under a withering fire gained him the highest military honour'. He was awarded the Victoria Cross.[444] Many others contain lengthy descriptions of the individual and his death.

The private memorials have inscriptions which show the mourning of the bereaved and their pride in the dead.

Many thousands of wreaths were laid at the memorials. At Ilfracombe, like many other places, wreaths at the unveiling expressed the grief of the living and attempts to pay tribute to the departed. Some were placed with messages of 'In ever loving memory of my dear boy, Reg, who gave his life for his King and Country, 1918, at the early age of 17 years, from his loving mother, 6 Hillside Terrace', 'In loving memory of I. H. and W. I. Barwick from their loving mother', 'In loving memory of my two grandsons, A.B.C. and H.W.G., from Mr and Mrs Cooper', 'In loving memory of two brave boys – Jack Edward and George Henry Rodd' and 'In loving and everlasting memory of our dear boys, William George and Edgar Stanley Conibear, from mam, dad, Hilda, Lily and Horace'. Likewise at Sidmouth where one wreath was 'In ever loving memory of our only dear boy, L. Cpl H. H. Skinner, who died in Mesopotamia December 2nd 1918, from his loving mother and father and sister Gladys, His memory lives in our hearts forever' and another had the simple message 'from an ever sorrowing mother'.

# CONCLUSION

# THE LEGACY OF REMEMBRANCE

As soon as the memorials were erected they assumed a unique place in each community. Not only had they become a focal point for the bereaved and Armistice Day commemorations but visiting dignitaries began to visit them. One such example took place in 1924 at Exeter when the mayor of Montdidier, the city's 'adopted town', laid a wreath at the monument.[445]

Whilst the monuments were being discussed and erected across the county there was another debate ensuing. Thousands of men had returned home to Devon to find that they were unemployed. Many of them were wounded, either physically or mentally. Prices had been steadily rising and the economic situation appeared to be deteriorating. Not surprisingly there were concerns over the support available to ex-servicemen and debate as to whether funds raised for monuments should not go the men themselves. This heightened the arguments for functional monuments. In 1922 Jan Stewer, Devon's local writer on dialect, included war monuments in one of his weekly pieces he wrote for the local press. He described one ex-serviceman who was selling matches as a war monument in himself.

'He was only a man. At laist, when I say a man, he had a-bin
a man one time or another, but he wad'n more 'n part of a one
now. He was a weesh poor maggit, sure nuff. There wad'n no
age to 'en. No more'n vive-an'-thirty I daun' reckon. But he
looked more like zempty-vive. I daun' spause all the blid in his
body wude full a pint mug, and if he'd a-changed his togs with
somebody's scarecrow he'd a-got the best o' the deal for certin.
I shude'n a-thort 'twas safe fer'n to go walking about, hardly,
cus a gude puff o' weend wude a-blawed 'n clane away. Jidging
by the looks a'wn, 'twas time to putt'n to bed and send fer the
docter. He looked about as much like a chap on his las' ligs as
ever I seed anybody'.[446]


The Devonians that erected the monuments and the
soldiers that survived the war have all long died. Before then
the memorials attained a place within society which was
kept through the 1920s and 1930s but the outbreak of war
in 1939 gave them an added poignancy and a renewed sense
of purpose. Many of the memorials had their inscriptions
amended in 1945 to take into account the new war dead.
Some added civilians to the lists because during the Second
World War deaths took place in Devon as well as abroad. In
the decades that have followed more names have been added
as new conflicts and war have taken place.

The monuments have shifted from being Great War
memorials to monuments of all war. And yet although nearly
a century has passed since the start of the First World War
the deaths in that war are greater than in all those that have
followed. The mass of inscribed names haunt the observer.
At the dedication of the war memorial at Chulmleigh one
local man told the crowd of those men who had died in the
war:

'They left their quiet homes in the countryside at the call of
arms to fight an arrogant and cruel enemy. They fought like
men, they suffered like men and they died like men. Most

families in the town had lost dear ones in the war. They bore their sorrow in silence and to them our deepest sympathy was extended. Those selfish people who were apt to exaggerate our little passing troubles should sometimes visit this cross and compare their sacrifice with that of the twenty-eight heroes from the parish who sacrificed everything that they possessed. I hope the names on the cross would be read frequently.'[447]

In 1920 the Bishop of Exeter said in Chagford that these war memorials were 'beautiful things if they were rightly understood and if they brought to the onlookers nobler thoughts, and if they stirred them to higher deeds and to wider conceptions of duty. If, after placing memorials, they forget the men and turned away from the sacrifice they made, and thought only of their own interest, their money or their pleasure, the memorials raised would stand as memorials to their shame.'[448] Another cleric, at the unveiling of Lifton's memorial said to the large crowd that when their generation passed away, a hundred years from then, the memorials would stand as silent reminders of how the shadow of the Great War had fallen across the whole country.[449]

The Wesleyan minister at Combe Martin looked to the future when he assisted in unveiling the memorial cross. He told his audience that future generations would have their struggles.

'Long after those present today had been laid beneath the sod that monument would be braving the storms, and as the waves on their shore followed one another, so generations would be succeeding them. Other feet than theirs would be passing along those paths and highways, and other eyes than theirs would be looking at the bronze tablet on which they had engraved those precious names. What would that pillar say to the generations that came after them? It had a message for them. They would be occupied in buying and selling and getting gain. They would know something about those perishable pleasures and short-lived cares that so much occupied our thoughts and hearts. But could we not put into them some thought that would give them bigger souls?'

He thought the message later generations would hear was the call to service.[450]

There is an echo to the words spoken and inscribed then. The history of their creation also has great power not just to inform but also to inspire. In the spring of 1926 the villagers of Trusham on the edge of Dartmoor witnessed an unusual spectacle. A war memorial was begun after eight years after the end of hostilities. It was finished in August and is perhaps the least artistically accomplished of all Devon's communal memorials. It takes the form of a tablet with two short pillars on either side. It is distinguished however by a second tablet, more detailed than the first, which shows it was not erected by a standard war memorial committee of the parish elite.

136. *The memorial erected at Trusham by former servicemen.*

137. *The Great War monument at Higher Tale.*

It tells us that this monument was built with the voluntary labour of eleven former servicemen in their free time on a site given by two other individuals with the stone, haulage and ironwork donated by a collection of other villagers. The engraving was done by a local woman. Their sense of duty

222

and determination to honour the dead is, arguably, more eloquently spoken than on any other Devon memorial. It was, as they said in the official programme, a 'silent witness to our labours of brotherhood in memory of those who fell'.[451]

Over the last ninety years various individuals have sought to repair and conserve some of Devon's Great War memorials, notably in Plymouth,[452] and occasional damage shocks Devonians, notably again in Plymouth most recently only a few years ago when four bronze panels were stolen from the Royal Naval monument on the Hoe. The daily journeys of most Devonians involve unsuspectingly passing by Great War memorials along roadsides, in churchyards and on the walls of buildings. They also lie embedded in the landscape as parks and halls and adorn our churches. To see one of the most moving of all one needs to travel to through the countryside to the hamlet of Higher Tale not far from the East Devon village of Payhembury. An unassuming stump of granite can be found nearly buried within the hedge. It is not handsome nor a particularly accomplished example of the stone mason's craft. The lettering is faint and the words are thus barely legible. With time the reader can learn that the stone was erected in loving memory of Henry and William Pratt who both died fighting in the Great War. This short obelisk could easily be mistaken for a discarded piece of farmyard granite. Yet this particular stone, and all other Great War monuments in Devon and elsewhere, act as silent reminders of another generation's service and sacrifice. They all have voices, some fainter than others, but only for those who allow themselves to pause and listen.

# ILLUSTRATION SOURCES

Frontispiece supplied by Graham Parnell; 8, Devon Record Office, Stoke Fleming, 1342A; 13, Devon Record Office, Churston Ferrers, 1235A-2PM3; 14, Devon Record Office, Salcombe Regis, 3232A/PM1; 16, Westcountry Studies Library, Harry Hems & Sons Scrapbooks; 34, *Western Times*, 10 September 1920; 35, Devon Record Office, Churston Ferrers, 1235A-2PM3; 36, Devon Record Office, Exwick 3336A-1/PZ; 49, *Western Weekly Mercury Illustrated*, 29 May 1920; 50, supplied by Graham Parnell; 64, Exeter Cathedral Archive; 65, supplied by Carole Herbert; 71–3, *Western Weekly Mercury Illustrated*, 9 October 1920, 10 January 1920, 24 January 1920; 82, supplied by Donald Grant; 123, Devon Record Office, unlisted collection of Herbert Read material; 124, *Western Weekly News*, 16 May 1923; 125, *Western Weekly News*, 29 May 1923; 126, Devon Record Office, Totnes 1579A/17.

# NOTES

1    The Imperial War Museum lists 971 First World War memorials on its website and this is only a portion of those that were erected. It is unlikely that the total figure will ever be known given the large number of private memorials that were created and not recorded.

2    In parishes across Devon there has been a great deal of research into the backgrounds of local men who died in the war. Many of them are in manuscript form in parish churches including, notably, Broadclyst. One of the most detailed studies to be published covers Tavistock, see Alex Mettler and Gerry Woodcock, *We will remember them* (Tavistock, 2003); www.Devonheritage.org cited on 1 October 2010 which looks at memorials across Devon; see North Devon Athenaeum, Brian Barrow's studies of soldiers of the great war in 50 parishes and three market towns in North Devon for information on the men who went to war in North Devon; see Barbara O'Kelly, 'Issues relating to the planning of First World War memorials: a South Devon case study', *The Devon Historian*, vol. 77, 2008, 37-47, for several communities in South Devon; Terry Leaman has done considerable work on Torbay's memorials as has Brian Mosley on those of Plymouth.

3    *Western Weekly News*, 11 October 1924.

4    *Western Times*, 5 August 1921.

5    *Western Times*, 24 March 1921.

6    *Express & Echo*, January 1917.

7    *Teignmouth Post*, 31 October 1919.

8    *Western Weekly Mercury Illustrated*, 24 July 1920. It eventually erected a cross.

9    Devon Record Office, 2954A-3/PP2-4.

10   *Western Weekly News*, 29 May 1923.

11   Devon Record Office, 1342A/PP, letter of Herbert Read, 23 May 1919.

12   Devon Record Office, 3232A/PM1.

13   *Totnes Times*, 17 May 1919.

14   Devon Record Office, 3420A-1/PW47.

15   *The Western Times*, 14 January 1920, 6 February 1920.

16   *Paignton Observer*, 25 November 1920. This was at the South Devon Granite Company's quarry at Swell Tor near Princetown: *Paignton Observer*, 30 June 1921.

17   Newton Abbot Museum, Box 96, letters of Courtney Pollock, 19 February 1921, 14 October 1921 and 23 September 1921..

18   *Teignmouth Post*, 7 November 1919.

19   *Express & Echo*, 7 August 1918.

20   *Western Morning News & Mercury*, 21 May 1923.

21   *Western Times*, 19 November 1920.

22   *Western Times*, 19 November 1920.

23   Another similar monument was erected to Thomas Dyke Acland at Killerton. This large granite cross was created in the late nineteenth century but is often assumed by visitors to the National Trust to be a war memorial.

24   *Express & Echo*, 10 October 1921.

25   *Totnes Times*, 2 July 1921.

26   *Express & Echo*, 12 July 1921.

27   *Western Times*, 1 April 1920.

28   Devon Record Office, 3004A/PM2.

29   *The Illustrated Western Weekly News*, 23 October 1920.

30   *The Illustrated Western Weekly News*, 18 November 1922.

31   *The Western Weekly News*, 10 May 1924; Plymouth & West Devon Record Office, 1676/130.

32   *Western Times*, 1 April 1920.

33   *Devon & Exeter Daily Gazette*, 3 November 1920.

34   *Teignmouth Post*, 31 December 1920, 23 January & 28 May 1920.

35   *Teignmouth Post*, 29 August 1919.

36   *Western Times*, 14 November 1921; *Ilfracombe Chronicle*, 19 November 1921.

37   *Express & Echo*, 12 October 1920.

38   *Western Times*, 25 May 1920.

39   *Devon & Exeter Daily Gazette*, 28 November 1919.

40   North Devon Record Office, 266-3/PW12/1-3. The idea for the hall was later withdrawn.

41   *Devon & Exeter Daily Gazette*, 30 October 1919.

42   Plymouth & West Devon Record Office, 737/144.

43   *Western Times*, 28 Feburary 1919.

44   *Paignton Observer*, 6 March 1919.

45   See *Dawlish Gazette*, 25 January, 1 & 15 February, 22 March, 5 & 12 April, 31 May, 7, 14 & 28 June, 5 & 12 July, 2 & 30 August 1919.

46   *Western Weekly Mercury*, 14 August 1920.

47   Devon Record Office, 1235A-2/PM3-4.

48   Devon Record Office, 1342A/PP330 & 302, & letter of Herbert Read, 7 November 1919.

49   *Western Times*, 28 February 1919.

50   North Devon Record Office, B380/7/1-2.

51   Devon Record Office, 3232A/PM1.

52   *Totnes Times*, 15 February 1919.

53   King, *Memorials*, 65.

54   *Devon & Exeter Daily Gazette*, 5 September 1919.

55   *Devon & Exeter Daily Gazette*, 31 July 1919; *Western Times*, 1 August 1919.

56   *Totnes Times*, 12 June 1920.

57   *Teignmouth Post*, 30 January 1920.

58   Bridget Cherry and Nikolaus Pevsner, *Devon* (1989), 797.

59   *Tiverton Gazette*, 25 March 1919.

60   *Tiverton Gazette*, 21 January 1919; *Western Times*, 20 January 1919.

61   *Tiverton Gazette*, 28 January 1919.

62   *Tiverton Gazette*, 22 April 1919.

63   *Devon & Exeter Daily Gazette*, 23 September 1919.

64   *Express & Echo*, 28 March 1920. One contributor wrote to the committee that 'in the opinion of most people it is out of place in English surroundings amid Western civilization. Surely a Celtic cross, such as many other towns are providing, would be a happier choice, far prettier and more in keeping with the cause': *The Illustrated Western Weekly News*, 3 April 1920.

65   *The Illustrated Western Weekly News*, 3 April 1920.

66    *Western Times*, 26 July 1919.
67    *Western Times*, 22 January 1920; *Express & Echo*, 21 January 1920.
68    *Western Times*, 15 October 1920.
69    *Western Times*, 29 October 1920.
70    *Totnes Times*, 8 February 1919.
71    *Plympton District Times*, 8 May 1924.
72    *Tiverton Gazette*, 7 October 1919.
73    Devon Record Office, Sandford A2/PG2.
74    *The Illustrated Western Weekly News*, 20 December 1919.
75    *Western Times*, 24 September 1920.
76    *Express & Echo*, 21 February 1921.
77    *Totnes Times*, 17 July 1920.
78    *Western Times*, 2 September 1920.
79    Devon Record Office, 3004A/PM2.
80    *The Illustrated Western Weekly News*, 16 August 1919.
81    *Devon & Exeter Daily Gazette*, 15, 20, 23, 25, 28 August 1919.
82    *Dawlish Gazette*, 28 January 1919.
83    *Totnes Times*, 2 April 1921.
84    *Devon & Exeter Daily Gazette*, 18 December 1919.
85    *Devon & Exeter Daily Gazette*, 18 May 1920.
86    *Express & Echo*, 10 October 1921.
87    *Totnes Times*, 2 July 1921.
88    *Ilfracombe Chronicle*, 7 May 1921.
89    *Western Times*, 3 December 1920.
90    *Express & Echo,* 13 March 1919, 19 April 1923; *Western Morning News & Mercury*, 1 February, 14 May & 6 November 1923; *Devon & Exeter Gazette*, 22 May 1924.
91    *Dawlish Gazette*, 21 February 1920.
92    *Western Evening Herald*, 14 March 1923.
93    *Devon & Exeter Daily Gazette*, 31 July 1919.
94    *Express & Echo*, 20 January 1920.
95    Devon Record Office, SR3232A/PM1.
96    *Totnes Times*, 8 February, 15 February, 1 March, 19 April, 26 April 1919.
97    *Tiverton Gazette*, 15 April 1919.
98    *The Illustrated Western Weekly News*, 1 march 1919.
99    *Devon & Exeter Daily Gazette*, 11 June 1920.
100   *Devon & Exeter Daily Gazette*, 10 September 1920.
101   *Devon & Exeter Daily Gazette*, 28 September 1920.
102   *Western Times*, 14 September 1920.

103  *Western Times*, 28 May 1920; *The Illustrated Western Weekly News*, 29 May 1920.

104  *Western Times*, 16 July 1920.

105  Devon Record Office, Sandford Add2/PG2 & Brampford Speke 305A-1/PB33-44.

106  *Express & Echo*, 20 October 1919.

107  *Plympton District Times*, 21 February 1924.

108  *Devon & Exeter Daily Gazette*, 27 July 1920.

109  *Devon & Exeter Daily Gazette*, 3 November 1920; *Express & Echo*, 2 November 1920.

110  *The Illustrated Western Weekly News*, 16 August 1919.

111  *Kingsbridge Gazette*, 27 June 1919.

112  *Totnes Times*, 20 December 1919.

113  An additional cost for Pollard was the foundation while Jenkins would also charge 12 shillings for a dozen letters.

114  Devon Record Office, 1342A/PP, letter of Herbert Read, 23 May 1919.

115  *The Illustrated Western Weekly News*, 17 May 1919.

116  *Totnes Times*, 20 December 1919; *Western Times*, 17 September 1920.

117  *Teignmouth Post*, 26 December 1919.

118  *Devon & Exeter Daily Gazette*, 31 October 1919.

119  *Devon & Exeter Daily Gazette*, 1 August 1919.

120  *Western Times*, 1 October 1920.

121  *Western Times*, 20 April 1922.

122  *The Illustrated Western Weekly News*, 1 march 1919.

123  *Devon & Exeter Daily Gazette*, 24 June 1919.

124  *The Illustrated Western Weekly News*, 15 February 1919.

125  Devon Record Office, 1579A-O/17/37-48; *The Illustrated Western Weekly News*, 1 March & 31 May 1919.

126  *The Illustrated Western Weekly News*, 31 May 1919.

127  *Tiverton Gazette*, 28 January 1919.

128  *Teignmouth Post*, 16 May 1919.

129  *Tiverton Gazette*, 4 February 1919.

130  *Tiverton Gazette*, 21 January 1919.

131  *Totnes Times*, 29 March 1919.

132  *Western Times*, 4 February 1920.

133  *The Illustrated Western Weekly News*, 1 March 1919.

134  *Western Times*, 3 March 1919.

135  *Express & Echo*, 9 March 1921.

136  *Totnes Times*, 6 September 1919.

137  *Express & Echo*, 13 October 1920.

138  *Teignmouth Post*, 21 February,11 July & 12 December 1919.

139  *Devon & Exeter Daily Gazette*, 2 December 1919.

140  *Devon & Exeter Daily Gazette*, 21 June 1919.

141  *The Illustrated Western Weekly News*, 21 February 1920.

142  *The Illustrated Western Weekly News*, 20 November 1920; *Sidmouth Herald*, 13 November 1920.

143  *Western Times*, 12 August 1919; *Paignton Observer*, 11 September 1919.

144  *The Illustrated Western Weekly News*, 26 July 1919

145  *Torquay Times*, 21 February 1919.

146  *Paignton Observer*, 21 August 1919.

147  *Western Times*, 7 February 1919.

148  *Western Times*, 3 March 1919.

149  *Western Times*, 28 March 1919

150  *Paignton Observer*, 30 January 1919.

151  *Ilfracombe Chronicle*, 15 March 1919.

152  Another built as a Victory Hall was that at Kenton: *Western Times*, 15 October 1920.

153  *Western Times*, 24 September 1920.

154  *Devon & Exeter Daily Gazette*, 28 May 1920; *Western Times*, 27 May 1920.

155  *Express & Echo*, 8 February 1921.

156  *Devon & Exeter Daily Gazette*, 10 June 1919.

157  *Express & Echo*, 18 October 1919.

158  *Paignton Observer*, 8 May 1919.

159  *Paignton Observer*, 10 April 1919.

160  *Kingsbridge Gazette*, 23 October 1925.

161  *Devon & Exeter Daily Gazette*, 5 November 1920; Westcountry Studies Library, Broadhembury parish magazines, 1919–1921. Colling's mother must have lived in Broadhembury after she left her birth-place of Exmouth: A. W. Ashby and revised by H. C. G. Matthew, 'Jesse Collings', *Oxford Dictionary of National Biography*.

162  *Devon & Exeter Daily Gazette*, 2 October 1920; *Western Times*, 5 & 7 October 1920; O'Kelly, 'Issues', 41.

163   *Devon & Exeter Daily Gazette*, 20 November 1919.

164  *Totnes Times*, 23 October 1920; *Western Times*, 15 October 1920.

165  *Express & Echo*, 25 August 1921.

166  *Devon & Exeter Daily Gazette,* 27 November 1919 & 3 November 1920.

167  *Devon & Exeter Daily Gazette*, 24 December 1919.

168 These include Combeinteignhead (*Teignmouth Post*, 23 May 1919) and Stoke Gabriel (*Totnes Times*, 29 March 1919).

169 *Devon & Exeter Daily Gazette*, 18 December 1919.

170 *Western Times*, 1 October 1920.

171 *The Illustrated Western Weekly News*, 3 May 1919.

172 *Ilfracombe Chronicle*, February 1921.

173 *Express & Echo*, 12 July 1921.

174 *Tiverton Gazette*, 23 May 1922.

175 *The Illustrated Western Weekly News*, 31 May 1919.

176 *The Illustrated Western Weekly News*, 16 August 1919

177 North Devon Record Office, R2379A/Z27; *Western Times*, 26 August 1921.

178 *Kingsbridge Gazette*, 6, 13 & 27 June 1919.

179 *Tiverton Gazette*, 13 May 1919; *Western Times*, 10 February 1920; Devon Record Office, R4/2/C12/103, 118-119, 125-7, 136-7, 142, 150-1, 209. The field was known as either Tucker's or Newcombe's Meadow.

180 Express & Echo, 29 January 1920.

181 Devon Record Office, 3248A-O/30/14/U; *Okehampton Post*, May 1925; *British Medical Journal*, 2: 851, 6 May 1926.

182 *Express & Echo*, 18 January 1921.

183 *Illustrated Western Weekly News*, 15 February 1919.

184 *Western Times*, 27 May 1920. Welcombe had four dead and erected a war memorial cross to them in 1920.

185 *Express & Echo*, 22 March 1920.

186 *The Illustrated Western Weekly News*, 25 October 1919.

187 Devon Record Office, 1342A/PP299-34, 252-98; *The Illustrated Western Weekly News*, 23 August 1919; *Totnes Times*, 27 March & 19 May 1920.

188 *Express & Echo*, 10 January 1921.

189 *Western Times*, 24 September 1920.

190 *Devon & Exeter Daily Gazette*, 2 November 1920.

191 *Totnes Times*, 18 December 1920. Mr Horn undertook the masonry work.

192 *Western Times*, 9 July 1920.

193 *Western Times*, 20 August 1920.

194 *Totnes Times*, 18 October 1919.

195 Devon Record Office, Salcombe Regis 3232A/PM1.

196 *Totnes Times*, 13 November 1920.

197 *Devon & Exeter Daily Gazette*, 16 September 1920; *Western Times*, 17 September 1920.

198 *The Illustrated Western Weekly News*, 4 October 1919.
199 *Express & Echo*, 22 March 1920.
200 *Western Times*, 6 February 1920.
201 *Express & Echo*, 3 November 1920.
202 *Teignmouth Post*, 7 February 1919; *The Illustrated Western Weekly News*, 31 May 1919.
203 *Totnes Times*, 5 February 1921.
204 Alan Borg, *War Memorials* (1991), 8.
205 Devon Record Office, 1235A-2/PM3-4.
206 M. S. Briggs, revised by Richard A. Fellows, 'Sir Reginald Theodore Blomfield', *Dictionary of National Biography*.
207 King, *Memorials of the Great War in Britain*, 150.
208 These were Mowbray of London, H. H. Martyn & Co. of Cheltenham, Cottier of Plymouth and F. Horn of Totnes.
209 *Totnes Times*, 11 June & 6 August 1921; Devon Record Office, 1579A-0/17/37-48. For the different descriptions of Mr Horn see Devon Record Office, 2001A/pw23.
210 King, *Memorials*, 154-5.
211 King, *Memorials of the Great War in Britain*, 154-5.
212 *Dawlish Gazette*, 2 January 1923.
213 *Devon & Exeter Daily Gazette*, 27 November 1919 & 2 November 1920; *Express & Echo*, 1 November 1920.
214 *Western Times*, 17 June 1921.
215 *Western Weekly Mercury Illustrated*, 3 July 1920; *Illustrated Western Weekly News*, 19 June 1920.
216 Borg, *War Memorials*, 7-9.
217 *Western Weekly Mercury Illustrated*, 6 March 1920.
218 *Devon & Exeter Daily Gazette*, 13 June 1919.
219 *Devon & Exeter Daily Gazette*, 17 June 1919.
220 *The Illustrated Western Weekly News*, 30 September 1921; *Tiverton Gazette*, 19 April 1921; *Western Times*, 6 May 1921; *Western Times*, 21 December 1921.
221 *Totnes Times*, 5 February 1921.
222 *Tiverton Gazette*, 2 August 1921.
223 *Totnes Times*, 9 August 1919.
224 *The Illustrated Western Weekly News*, 17 April 1920.
225 *Devon & Exeter Daily Gazette*, 9 September 1920.
226 *Devon & Exeter Daily Gazette*, 3 September 1920.
227 *Devon & Exeter Daily Gazette*, 27 July 1920.
228 *The Illustrated Western Weekly News*, 11 September 1920.
229 *The Illustrated Western Weekly News*, 8 May 1920.

230  *The Illustrated Western Weekly News*, 15 May 1920.

231  *Express & Echo*, 21 February 1921.

232  *Devon & Exeter Daily Gazette*, 13 June 1919.

233  *Devon & Exeter Daily Gazette*, 1 November 1919.

234  *Totnes Times*, 29 January 1921.

235  *Express & Echo*, 14 March 1921.

236  *Devon & Exeter Daily Gazette*, 28 November 1919.

237  *The Illustrated Western Weekly News*, 4 October 1919.

238  *Western Times*, 18 April 1921.

239  *Western Times*, 10 September 1920.

240  *Western Weekly Mercury Illustrated*, 3 July 1920.

241  *Western Weekly Mercury Illustrated*, 7 February 1920.

242  *Western Times*, 17 June 1921.

243  *Western Times*, 15 October 1920.

244  *The Illustrated Western Weekly News*, 8 November 1919.

245  *Western Times*, 17 June 1921.

246  *Devon & Exeter Daily Gazette*, 9 September 1920.

247  *Devon & Exeter Daily Gazette*, 17 September 1920; *Western Times*, 17 September 1920; *Western Weekly Mercury Illustrated*, 1 May 1920.

248  *Express & Echo*, 6 June 1921.

249  Newton Abbot Museum, Box 96, letter of Coleridge White, 29 September 1920.

250  Devon Record Office, 1342A/PP, letter of Herbert Read, 23 May 1919.

251  *Devon & Exeter Gazette*, 24 December 1919.

252  Exeter Cathedral Archive, box of correspondence, letter of E. H. Harbottle, 16 December 1921.

253  Exeter Cathedral Archive, Dean & Chapter Minute Book 4, page 490, meeting of 21 December 1918.

254  *Express & Echo*, 15 February 1919.

255  *The Western Times*, 17 January 1919; *Tiverton Gazette*, 25 February 1919.

256  *Express & Echo*, 2 July 1919.

257  *Express & Echo*, 2 July 1919.

258  *The Western Times, 19 August 1919.*

259  *The Illustrated Western Weekly News*, 2 August 1919.

260  Exeter Cathedral Archive, Dean & Chapter Minute book 5, page 42, meeting of 26 July 1919.

261  Exeter Cathedral Archive, Dean & Chapter Minute book 5, page 75, meeting of 15 November 1919, page 87, meeting of 20 December

1919, page 223, meeting of 26 March 1921; *Devon & Exeter Daily Gazette*, 24 December 1919.
262  *The Western Times*, 16 August 1919.
263  *The Western Times*, 26 July 1919.
264  Exeter Cathedral Archive, Dean & Chapter Minute book 5, page 129, meeting of 15 May 1920 and page 130, meeting of 22 May 1920.
265  *The Times*, 17 May 1921.
266  Tim Skelton, Gerald Gliddon and Gavin Stamp, *Lutyens and the Great War* (2009), 112.
267  *Express & Echo*, 7, 14, 21 May 1921.
268  *Crediton Chronicle*, April 1923; *The Times*, 8 December 1919, 11 August 1924, 13 March 1945.
269  *Express & Echo*, 27 March 1921.
270  *Express & Echo*, 28 March 1920.
271  *Teignmouth Post*, 2 April 1920.
272  *Plympton District Times*, 8 May 1924; *Western Weekly News,* 10 May 1924; Reginald Blomfield, *Memoirs of an architect* (1932), 183.
273  Borg, *War Memorials*, 4, 86-7.
274  *Ilfracombe Chronicle*, 22 February 1919 & 15 March 1919.
275  *Totnes Times*, 6 September 1919.
276  *Western Times*, 16 July 1920.
277  *Western Times*, 1 October 1920.
278  *Tiverton Gazette*, 14 January 1919.
279  *Express & Echo*, 29 March 1920.
280  *Express & Echo*, 12 July 1921.
281  *Western Morning News & Mercury*, 30 July 1924.
282  *The Times*, 30 July 1924.
283  *Western Weekly Mercury Illustrated*, 17 July 1920.
284  *Plymouth Evening Herald* & *Western Evening Herald*, 14 March 1923.
285  King, *Memorials*, 149.
286  *Illustrated Western Weekly News*, 20 November 1920 & 21 February 1920.
287  *Illustrated Western Weekly News*, 2 August 1919.
288  *Western Times*, 31 January 1919.
289  *Express & Echo*, 21 April 1921; Blomfield, *Architect*, 183-4.
290  *Western Weekly News*, 10 May 1924.
291  *Paignton Observer*, 16 January 1919.
292  *Western Times*, 3 March 1919.

293  Borg, *War Memorials*, 99-100.

294  *Western Times*, 13 July 1920.

295  *Kingsbridge Gazette*, 6, 13 & 27 June 1919, 25 October 1925; *Totnes Times*, 21 November 1925. In August 1925 a question was asked in a meeting of the urban district council about the memorial and councillors were told that the base had been ordered but was not expected to arrive for a further 3 months: *Kingsbridge Gazette*, 21 August 1925. Also, that spring the Ministry of Health sanctioned reasonable expenses for the base of the memorial: Devon Record Office, R9/4/C6, meeting of urban district council, 5 May 1925.

296  Newton Abbot Museum, Box 96, letter of Courtenay Pollock, 6 September 1920.

297  Newton Abbot Museum, Box 96, two letters of Courtenay Pollock, 16 August 1921.

298  Information supplied by Felicity Cole, curator of Newton Abbot Town and GWR Museum.

299  Newton Abbot Museum, Box 96, letters of Courtenay Pollock, 9 October 1920 & 4 October 1921.

300  *Ilfracombe Chronicle*, 15 November 1924. The design was announced two and a half years earlier: *Ilfracombe Chronicle*, 1 July 1922.

301  Newton Abbot Museum, Box 96, letter of Courtenay Pollock, 8 August 1922.

302  *Western Weekly News*, 26 May 1923.

303  Plymouth Local Studies Library, notes on the Royal Marines' Monument.

304  *Express & Echo*, 1 March 1919; *Devon & Exeter Daily Gazette*, 23 July 1923.

305  *The Western Times*, 26 July 1919; *Express & Echo*, 24 July 1923; Smithsonian Museum, John Angel papers, letters of 17 March and 25 July 1919.

306  *Express & Echo*, 4 May 1922, 21 July 1923.

307  *Express & Echo*, 16 August 1919.

308  Owen's son-in-law was the editor of the *Devon & Exeter Daily Gazette*.

309  *Devon & Exeter Daily Gazette*, 23 September 1919.

310  *Exeter & Devon Daily Gazette*, 20 August 1919; *Express & Echo*, 14 February 1920.

311  *Express & Echo*, 24 July 1923. Angel reportedly had assistance from two Exeter architects, Sidney Greenslade and R. M. Chalice.

312  *The Times*, 2 May 1922; *Devon & Exeter Daily Gazette*, 16 May 1922.
313  *Express & Echo*, 24 July 1923.
314  *Express & Echo*, 24 July 1923.
315  *Express & Echo*, 4 May 1922 & 24 July 1923.
316  *Express & Echo*, 12 May 1920.
317  Westcountry Studies Library, Exeter City Council minutes, Estates Committee 30 March & 11 May 1920; *Express & Echo*, 23 May 1919; *Devon & Exeter Daily Gazette*, 18 September 1919; Smithsonian Museum, letters of John Bennet, 27 April, 4 May and 14 May 1920.
318  *Express & Echo*, 17 October 1919, 3 January 1920.
319  *Express & Echo*, 24 July 1923.
320  *The Western Times*, 26 July 1919.
321  *Express & Echo*, 24 July 1923; *Devon & Exeter Daily Gazette*, 2 October 1923.
322  Smithsonian Museum, Letters of William Morris, 28 August 1922 & 28 June 1923.
323  *Express & Echo*, 7 February & 16 June 1923.
324  *The Times*, 25 July 1923.
325  *Express & Echo*, 24 July 1923.
326  Smithsonian Museum, John Angel Papers, letters of 2 August & 23 October 1923.
327  *Exeter Flying Post*, 23 July 1857. The monument claims it was erected in 1860.
328  The monument was made by Edward Richardson of Melbury Terrace, London.
329  Exeter Cathedral Archives, Dean & Chapter minute book, July 1920.
330  Exeter Cathedral Archives, Dean & Chapter minute book, 12 January 1920, 3 June 1920, July 1920.
331  *The Western Times*, 26 July 1921.
332  *The Western Times*, 21 & 27 June 1921. Also, the *Express & Echo*, 20 June 1921.
333  *The Western Times*, 26 July 1921.
334  See *The Greater Love: Poems of Remembrance* (London, 1919) .
335  *The Western Times*, 27 July 1921.
336  *The Times*, 27 July 1936.
337  Among them is a stone tablet of the Great War to the men of the Devonshire Regiment Territorial Force Battalions who died while serving in India, Mesopotamia, Palestine and elsewhere and another

to the three Devonshire Regiment Cyclist Battalions who gave their
lives. In May 1924 a marble tablet was unveiled in honour of those
of the Royal First Devon Yeomanry who died in the First World
War. There is also a marble wall memorial to the 124 local men of
the Royal First Devon Yeomanry who died in service during the war:
*Devon & Exeter Gazette*, 26 May 1924.

338 *Western Times*, 27 October 1922.
339 *Devon & Exeter Daily Gazette*, 8 January 1917. See also the oak
centerpiece for the altar at Highampton.
340 *Devon & Exeter Daily Gazette*, 12 September 1919; John Scott,
*Towers and Bells of Devon* (Exeter, 2007), II, 20. See also Buckerell
for a war memorial bell.
341 *Express & Echo*, 22 July 1921.
342 *Tiverton Gazette*, 4 November 1919.
343 *The Illustrated Western Weekly News*, 31 May 1919.
344 *The Illustrated Western Weekly News*, 25 November 1922.
345 *Western Times*, 21 May 1920.
346 *Devon & Exeter Daily Gazette*, 26 October 1920; *Western Times*,
26 October 1920.
347 *Express & Echo*, 14 February 1920.
348 *Express & Echo*, 23 February 1920.
349 *Devon & Exeter Daily Gazette*, 25 June 1920.
350 *Devon & Exeter Daily Gazette*, 24 May 1920.
351 *Express & Echo*, 3 October 1921.
352 Devon Record Office, 1269A/PW3; *Express & Echo*, 15 March
1921.
353 *Devon & Exeter Daily Gazette*, 26 July 1920; *Teignmouth Post*, 20
February 1920.
354 *Western Times*, 17 November 1922; *Illustrated Western Weekly
News*, 25 November 1922.
355 *Devon & Exeter Daily Gazette*, 26 October 1920; *Western Times*,
26 October 1920.
356 *Devon & Exeter Daily Gazette*, 12 November 1919.
357 *Devon & Exeter Daily Gazette*, 16 November 1920.
358 *Express & Echo*, 7 September 1921.
359 John Jones, *The Story of a Window* (leaflet prepared by Broadclyst
Local History Society for Broadclyst Parish Church, 2004). The
window is the work of Clayton & Bell: I am grateful to Mr Jones
for this information; the windoww to the war dead and Captain
Whitaker were granted faculties in 1919: Devon Record Office,
3594A-99/PW34-5.

360 *The Illustrated Western Weekly News*, 29 November 1919; *The Church of Allhallows Ringmore* (Ringmore, no date given), 22.

361 The north and south walls are dedicated as war memorials. Other panels were later added to the north transept: *Holy Trinity Church Exmouth* (no date or place of publication given), 5.

362 *Devon & Exeter Daily Gazette*, 28 June 1920.

363 *Tiverton Gazette*, 16 August 1921.

364 *Tiverton Gazette*, 23 May 1922.

365 *Western Times*, 1 October 1920; *Devon & Exeter Daily Gazette*, 29 September 1920. Prynne was also responsible for the church memorial at Ashburton: *Totnes Times*, 9 August 1919.

366 *Tiverton Gazette*, 16 August 1921.

367 Devon Record Office, 3420A-1/PW47.

368 *Devon & Exeter Daily Gazette*, 28 October 1920.

369 *Devon & Exeter Daily Gazette*, 28 June 1920.

370 *Western Times*, 2 October 1921; *Crediton Chronicle*, 19 & 26 November 1921.

371 *Express & Echo*, 12 April 1919.

372 Cheriton Bishop was another village which discussed a memorial clock: Devon Record Office, 132A/PP12-15.

373 *Devon & Exeter Daily Gazette*, 28 November 1919.

374 *Tiverton Gazette*, 25 March 1919.

375 *Western Times*, 6 August 1920. The clock was installed by August.

376 *Totnes Times*, 20 December 1919, 19 November 1921.

377 *Devon & Exeter Daily Gazette*, 19 August 1919; *Western Times*, 6 June 1921.

378 Devon Record Office, Sandford Add2/PG2.

379 *Dawlish Gazette,* 28 January 1919.

380 *The Illustrated Western Weekly News*, 27 December 1919.

381 *The Western Times*, 21 July 1920; *Devon & Exeter Daily Gazette*, 21 July 1920; *Express & Echo*, 21 July 1920.

382 Devon Record Office, 1417A-2/PW15-16.

383 *The Illustrated Western Weekly News*, 29 November 1919. Lt Col. Humphrey Dene died in January 1948: *The Times*, 22 January 1948.

384 *Totnes Times*, 24 April 1920.

385 *Western Times*, 13 & 16 July 1920.

386 There is also one at Kenn.

387 *Express & Echo*, 14 May 1917.

388 *Express & Echo*, 15 July 1922.

389 Westcountry Studies Library, Exeter City Council minutes, Estates Committee 30 March 1920, 31 May 1921.
390 Westcountry Studies Library, Exeter City Council minutes, Estates Committee 10 May 1920.
391 *Express & Echo*, 10 & 13 July 1920; *The Western Times*, 14 July 1920.
392 Westcountry Studies Library, Exeter City Council minutes, Estates Committee, 3 October 1922.
393 Arthur Charles Ellis, *An Historical Survey of Torquay From the Earliest Times* (Torquay, 1930), 476.
394 *The Illustrated Western Weekly News*, 1 February 1919.
395 *The Illustrated Western Weekly News*, 1 March 1919.
396 *The Western Times*, 30 April 1921.
397 *The Devonian Year Book 1922*, 48-9, taken from the *Western Weekly News; The Western Times*, 11 November 1921.
398 *Western Times*, 13 July 1920.
399 *Western Times*, 27 May 1920; *Express & Echo*, 20 May 1921. At Appledore Lieutenant Douglas Smith unveiled the memorial because his father, who had been the largest donor, was unable to be present: *Express & Echo*, 13 July 1920.
400 *Western Times*, 23 May 1921; *Teignmouth Post*, 15 October 1920.
401 *Western Times*, 17 May 1921.
402 *The Illustrated Western Weekly News*, 7 August 1920.
403 *Western Weekly Mercury Illustrated*, 14 August 1920.
404 *Express & Echo*, 12 August 1920.
405 *The Times*, obituaries, 24 June 1936 & 10 July 1930.
406 *Express & Echo*, 19 July 1921; This appears to have been his standard speech to give at war memorial dedications. For Littlehempston see *Totnes Times*, 16 October 1920, Littlehempston at *Western Times*, 11 October 1920.
407 *Express & Echo*, 28 June 1920. He made similar comments at Dunsford later that year: *Express & Echo*, 13 December 1920.
408 *Express & Echo*, 13 December 1920.
409 *Plympton District Times*, 8 May 1924.
410 Todd Gray, *Blackshirts in Devon* (Exeter, 2006), 4, 9.
411 *Totnes Times*, 9 July 1921.
412 *Teignmouth Post*, 28 January 1921.
413 *The Illustrated Western Weekly News*, 30 October 1920.
414 *Paignton Observer*, 5 June 1919.
415 *Paignton Observer*, 3 July 1919.
416 *Paignton Observer*, 5 June 1919.

417   *Paignton Observer*, 1 January 1920.

418   *Totnes Times*, 6 September 1919.

419   *Western Times*, 16 & 23 July 1920.

420   *Western Times*, 10 March 1922.

421   *Western Times*, 3 March 1919.

422   *Express & Echo*, 11 January 1917.

423   *Exeter Flying Post*, 13 January 1917. See also *Devon & Exeter Daily Gazette*, 11 January 1917.

424   *Express & Echo*, 22-8 February 1917.

425   *The Times*, 3 & 16 October 1916.

426   *Paignton Observer*, 10 July 1919. This was at St Michael's. Another, with a white crucifix, was at All Saint's Church in Torquay late in 1917: *Torquay Times*, 2 November 1917.

427   *Devon & Exeter Daily Gazette*, 24 November 1916. Boggis would become vicar of St Edmund's Church in 1945. He died at Pinhoe in 1951: *The Times*, 13 November 1951; R. J. Edmund Boggis, *Praying for the Dead* (1913).

428   *The Western Times*, 28 February 1917.

429   *The Western Times*, 3 March 1917.

430   Devon Record Office, 2738addA/PV1-2 & 6854b. In the church accounts there is an entry for money raised for the war shrine in January 1917 whereas from November 1918 onwards the references are to a war memorial: Devon Record Office, 2738A/add/pw1, entries for 7 January 1917, 17 November 1918, 3 August, 2, 9, 16 November 1919.

431   *The Western Times*, 1 May 1922.

432   *The Illustrated Western Weekly News*, 2 October 1920.

433   *The Western Times*, 2 & 11 April 1921; *The Times*, 11 April 1921.

434   Plymouth Local Studies Library, W. J. Power, 'A Layman's View of Some Plymouth Churches' (1977).

435   *Devon & Exeter Daily Gazette*, 13 November 1920.

436   *The Illustrated Western Weekly News*, 1 March 1919

437   *Totnes Times*, 3 September 1921. I am grateful to Reverend Tim Deacon for confirming the crucifix was given to All Saint's Church when St Peter's was closed.

438   *Dawlish Gazette*, 12 March 1921.

439   One of the exceptions is the roll of honour at the Jewish synagogue in Plymouth on which was written 'Roll of Honour, for King and Country, Names of those who have joined His Majesty's forces from the Plymouth Hebrew Congregation'.

440   Wilfred Owen's poem was published later.

441   Devon Record Office, 1342A/PP, letter of Herbert Read, 7 November 1919.
442   I am grateful to Graham Parnell for supplying this inscription.
443   A school monument now at the church of St John the Evangelist in Plymouth is inscribed '. . . in the supreme struggle against injustice and inhumanity'.
444   Devon Record Office, 1269A-6/PW5.
445   *Western Weekly News*, 11 October 1924.
446   *Illustrated Western Weekly News*, 11 November 1922.
447   *Western Times*, 10 September 1920.
448   *Western Times*, 20 August 1920.
449   *Western Times*, 6 February 1920.
450   *Ilfracombe Chronicle*, 7 May 1921.
451   Devon Record Office, 1269A-6/PW3.
452   *Plymouth Evening Herald*, 28 September 2002 & 8 November 2003.

# INDEX